THE GIFT OF
THOMAS JOSEPH WHITE
M.D., L.H.D., F.A.C.P.
TO THE LIBRARY OF
CABRINI COLLEGE
1981

Presidents
Who Have Known
Me

BY GEORGE E. ALLEN

SIMON AND SCHUSTER

NEW YORK

MANUFACTURED IN THE UNITED STATES OF AMERICA
AMERICAN BOOK–KNICKERBOCKER PRESS, INC., NEW YORK, N. Y.

DEDICATION

I HAVE never had a book dedicated to me. If an author were to pay me this high honor, I should consider myself duty bound to buy many copies for myself and friends. This would be no more than decent.

It is the usual procedure to dedicate a book to somebody "without whose help this literary achievement would have been impossible." There is already enough talk about this book being impossible. I am not going to bother with this convention. It is not sufficiently forward-looking.

To the following few friends and associates, who haven't helped at all with the writing but whose help with the selling is earnestly requested, I dedicate this volume.

Abernethy, Thomas G.
Acheson, Dean
Adam, Malcolm
Adams, Fred B.
Adams, Joe
Allen, Charlie
Allyn, Arthur C.
Alvord, Ellsworth, C.
Anderson, Clinton P.
Anderson, W. H.
Andrews, Frank L.
Arvey, J. M.
Austin, Warren
Axman, Clarence

Babcock, Irving B.
Babson, Roger W.
Baird, Bruce
Balaban, Barney
Balyeat, Hal B.
Barnes, James M.

Barringer, L. T.
Barron, Carter T.
Baruch, Bernard M.
Bazelon, David L.
Beale, Leonard T.
Bean, Louis
Beck, Dave
Becker, Neal Dow
Beebe, Raymond N.
Beise, S. Clark
Bell, Daniel W.
Benton, William
Berns, John
Bierwith, John E.
Bingham, Hiram
Biow, Milton H.
Black, C. R.
Black, Eugene R.
Black, Kenneth E.
Blees, William A.
Bodine, William W.

Bodman, Harry
Boshell, Edward O.
Bowles, Chester
Boyle, William M., Jr.
Brace, Howard J.
Brandon, Jerry
Bridges, Styles
Briggs, Milton
Brinley, Charles E.
Broderick, David
Brower, H. W.
Brown, Harry L.
Brownell, Herbert
Browning, Gordon
Bruce, James
Budd, Edward G.
Bullitt, Orville H.
Burke, John
Burke, Vincent C.
Burton, James C.

DEDICATION

Caffey, Frank
Caldwell, Louis
Call, Asa
Callery, Francis A.
Campbell, Alexander M.
Capper, Arthur
Carr, Harry
Carroll, James J.
Carter, Amon
Cavagnaro, James F.
Chapman, Oscar L.
Chow, Albert K.
Christenberry, Robert
Clancy, Robert H.
Clark, Bennett Champ
Clark, John C.
Clark, Tom C.
Clarke, Dwight L.
Clarke, Lewis L.
Cleary, William C.
Clegg, Hugh H.
Clement, Martin W.
Cobb, Ty
Cochran, W. Kent
Cohen, Benjamin A.
Colmer, William
Connally, Tom
Cook, Donald
Cooper, Jere
Cord, E. L.
Corrigan, Emmett
Costello, William C.
Cox, Oscar
Cox, Willard, R.
Coy, Wayne
Craig, John W.
Cronin, William F.
Cross, Julian G.
Crowley, Leo T.
Cruickshank, Herbert W.
Crum, Bartley
Crump, Ed
Cummings, Walter J.
Curran, Edward M.
Curran, Thomas J.

D'Alesandro, Thomas
Daley, William R.
Darling, C. Coburn
Davis, Chester C.
Dawson, Donald S.
Day, H. Mason
Deetjen, Rudolph H.
Delano, Preston
Delmar, Charles
Dempsey, John J.
Diemand, John A.
Diggs, Marshall R.
Dodds, Chauncey Y.

Dolph, W. B.
Donaldson, Jesse M.
Donnelly, Walter J.
Dougherty, James L.
Downey, Sheridan
Doyle, John H.
Dwyer, Ed

Eastland, James O
Eaton, Cyrus C.
Eaton, Harry
Eben, S. N.
Edmonstone, Neil
Eisenhower, Edgar N.
Eisenhower, Milton
Ellis, George A.
Emanuel, Victor
Emerson, Guy
Eppley, Gene
Ethridge, Mark
Eurich, Alvin C.
Evans, Thomas
Ewing, Esmond
Eynon, Edward

Fahey, John H.
Faricy, William T.
Ferguson, Abner
Ferguson, Homer
Field, Marshall
Finlay, J. J.
Fisher, Charles T., Jr.
Fitzpatrick, Paul
Flanagan, Horace C.
Fleger, Philip A.
Fleming, Philip B.
Fleming, Robert V.
Flook, William M.
Foley, Edward H., Jr.
Folger, W. P.
Foote, F. W.
Ford, Peyton
Fotheringham, M. C.
Foy, Norman
Francis, C. I.
Fretwell, Elbert K.
Froelich, William J.
Frye, Jack
Fuller, Walter D.

Gannett, Frank E.
Gannon, Charles
Garey, Eugene L.
Garni, Adolph
George, Walter F.
Gerard, Sumner
Giannini, L. Mario
Gibbons, Stephen B.
Gibson, Harvey

Gillette, Guy M.
Gillis, Don
Glass, Fred
Goldman, Albert
Goodloe, John
Goodwillie, Edward
Gordon, Max
Gosden, Freeman F.
Gowen, James E.
Grace, Eugene Peter
Grady, L. Vaughan
Graham, Wallace H.
Green, Theodore Francis
Green, Thomas D.
Green, William L.
Grew, Joseph C.
Griffith, Clark C.
Grimm, Peter
Gruenther, Alfred M.
Gruhn, A. V.
Guerrini, Ugo E.
Gund, George
Gunderson, Harvey J.
Gunn, George
Gurley, Fred G.

Hancock, Wayne W.
Harding, Victor Hunt
Hardy, Lamar
Hargrett, Felix
Hargrove, R. H.
Harl, Maple T.
Harriman, W. Averell
Harrison, Earl G.
Hartmeyer, L. Irwin
Hartsfield, William
Hasler, Frederick E.
Hassett, William D.
Hatch, Carl
Haworth, Ross
Hayden, Carl
Head, Walter W.
Hearst, William R., Jr.
Hecht, Rudolf S.
Heincke, William
Helm, Harold H.
Henderson, Leon
Herrington, A. W.
Hertz, John
Higbie, Carlton M.
High, S. J.
Hilbert, Webb
Hill, Arthur M.
Hill, Ashby
Hill, George
Hill, John W.
Hill, Lester
Hinckley, Robert
Hise, Harley

DEDICATION

Hoey, Clyde R.
Hoffman, Paul G.
Holtzoff, Alexander
Honeycutt, Jess
Hoover, J. Edgar
Hope, F. M.
Hopkins, John Jay
Houghton, Amory
Houston, Frank K.
Huggins, William L.
Hughes, Everett S.
Hughes, Harold
Hunneman, William C., Jr.
Hunt, Lester C.
Husbands, Sam H.

Ironside, Fred A.

Jackson, James A.
Jackson, Robert
Jackson, Robert H.
Jagoe, Armiger L., Jr.
James, Lee Warren
Jelleff, Frank R.
Jenkins, V. H.
Johnson, Christian A.
Johnson, Edwin C.
Johnson, George D.
Johnson, Howard
Johnson, J. Monroe
Johnson, John B.
Johnson, Louis
Johnson, Lyndon B.
Johnson, Olin D.
Johnson, Robert L.
Johnston, Felton M.
Johnston, Henry Alan
Jones, Marvin
Jones, Pete
Jones, Walker
Jorgenson, Arnold

Kaufman, Joseph David
Kaufmann, Arthur C.
Keane, Michael, Jr.
Keech, Richmond B.
Kefauver, Estes
Kemper, James Scott
Kerr, Robert S.
Kilgore, Harley M.
Killion, George
Kimball, Dan A.
Kindl, Carl
King, Krryn
Kirchner, Walter
Kirwan, Michael J.
Kleberg, Richard M.
Knowland, William F.
Kridel, Frank

Krienler, Max
Kurtz, William Fulton

Land, Emory S.
Landa, Alfons B.
Landis, James M.
Lannan, J. Patrick
Lapham, Roger D.
Lauderdale, James W.
Lawrence, David
Laws, Bolitha J.
Leary, Dennis W.
Lee, Josh
Lehman, Herbert H.
Lehman, Robert
Leigh, Carl G.
Lemon, James
Lennon, Thomas
Less, William L., II
Levering, E. W., Jr.
Leverone, Nathaniel
Levy, Robert J.
Lincoln, Leroy A.
Lindheimer, Benjamin F.
Lloyd, Humphrey
Lombardo, Guy
Loos, Karl D.
Loughin, Charles A.
Lounsbury, Herbert
Lynn, David

MacLeish, Archibald
McCabe, James H.
McCance, Pressly H.
McCarran, Pat
McCarthy, Clem
McCracken, Robert T.
McCracken, Wm. P., Jr.
McDonald, Stewart
McEvoy, William J.
McFarland, Ernest W.
McGrannery, James
McGrath, J. Howard
McGuire, Matthew F.
McIlwain, Sam D.
McIntire, Ross T.
McIntosh, Russell
McKeller, Kenneth
McLaren, Jock
McNutt, Paul V.
Mack, Walter
Macquire, W. G.
Magnuson, Warren G.
Mallon, H. Neil
Malone, George W.
Manning, Fred
Markham, James E.
Marshall, John
Martin, David

Martin, Wm. McChesney, Jr
Mason, Guy
Mau, Haveth
Maverick, Maury
Maybank, Burnet R.
Mead, James M.
Meigs, Merrill C.
Mein, W. W.
Merriam, John E.
Milde, Walter
Miller, Justin
Miller, Paul
Miller, William M.
Mitchell, William D.
Mize, Sidney C.
Moffett, James
Mogensen, Walter A.
Moore, L. Gardner
Moore, Robert
Moran, Robert Pete
Morgan, Thomas F.
Morgan, Tom
Morgan, William A.
Morris, Edger
Morrison, Fred
Mosher, Orville M.
Mulligan, Minot C.
Mulligan, Ralph C.
Murphy, Charles S.
Murray, Owen M.
Murray, Philip
Murray, Wallace
Myers, Francis J.

Namm, Benjamin H.
Needham, Maurice H.
Neeley, Matthew M.
Nelson, Donald M.
Newhouse, R. J.
Niles, David K.
Noble, Edward
Nolan, James
Norris, Ernest E.
Nunan, Joseph D., Jr.

O'Connell, Ambrose
O'Conor, Herbert R.
Odlum, Floyd
O'Dwyer, William
O'Hara, Thomas A.
O'Mahoney, Joseph C.
Oliphant, Charles

Pace, Frank, Jr.
Page, Frank C.
Paley, William
Palmer, Raymond
Parker, John E.
Parr, Henry A., III

DEDICATION

Parran, Thomas
Parsons, J. Lester
Patman, Wright
Patterson, R. C., Jr.
Patterson, Robert P.
Patton, Thomas
Paty, B. F.
Paul, Arthur
Payne, Herbert A.
Pepper, George Wharton
Perelle, Charles W.
Perlman, Philip B.
Peurifoy, John E.
Phillips, Harry
Pierce, Dan
Pierotti, Roland
Pierson, Warren Lee
Pine, David A.
Pink, Louis H.
Prettyman, E. Barrett
Price, Byron
Price, Karl R.
Prindeville, Thomas J.
Pruitt, Raymond S.
Pryor, Sam

Quale, Oliver A., Jr.

Ramspeck, Carl
Reece, Carroll
Reece, Ted
Reed, McKay
Reed, Stanley F
Reilly, Dan W.
Reinhardt, Henry B.
Reinsch, J. Leonard
Reynolds, George
Richardson, Seth W.
Richardson, Sid
Richardson, W. Edwin
Riley, George V.
Roach, William Neale
Roberts, Cliff
Roberts, Isaac W.
Roberts, Owen
Robertson, Gordon H.
Rockefeller, William
Roosevelt, Franklin D., Jr.
Royall, Kenneth C.
Royce, Steven W.
Russell, Richard B.
Russell, Stanley
Rust, H. L., Jr.

Sachs, Alfred T.
Sauter, James

Sawyer, Charles
Sayler, Henry B.
Schaffer, William I.
Schenck, Nicholas
Schiendorf, J. M.
Schoeneman, George J.
Schram, Emil
Schuck, Arthur A.
Scully, Thomas P.
Seal, Elwood H.
Sheppard, James C.
Shipley, Charles R.
Shor, Toots
Shouse, James D.
Shriver, George
Shriver, William C.
Six, Robert F.
Skouras, Spyros P.
Slater, Ellis D.
Smallwood, Robert B.
Smarr, Ben
Smith, Arthur Clarendon
Smith, C. Harry
Smith, C. R.
Smith, J. P.
Snyder, Carl
Snyder, Howard
Sommers, Paul B.
Souers, Sidney W.
Sparkman, John J.
Sprague, Mortimer E.
Stanton, Frank
Stennis, John C.
Stephens, Harold M.
Steudel, Arthur W.
Stuart, Charles B.
Stuart, Sam
Studebaker, John
Sturgis, Henry S.
Sullens, Fred
Sullivan, John L.
Swanson, L. Clarke
Swope, Herbert B.
Symington, W. Stuart

Tamm, Edward A.
Tancer, Forrest
Taylor, Wayne C.
Thomas, Eugene
Thomas, Fay M.
Thomas, Fred L.
Thomas, Norman
Thornett, G. M.
Tobin, Dan
Tobin, Maurice J.
Tolson, Clyde A.

Trammell, Niles
Tripp, Juan T.
Truitt, Max O'Rell
Tuckerman, Walter R.
Tunney, Gene
Tydings, Millard

Vandenburg, Arthur
Vanderbilt, Alfred G.
Van Orman, F. Harold

Wadsworth, Daniel V.
Wallace, Lew
Wallcott, Jesse
Waller, John R.
Walsh, Jack
Walsh, Tom
Warren, Fuller
Warwick, C. H.
Washington, George T.
Watson, Thomas J.
Weakly, Frank E.
Weinberg, Sidney
Weiss, Seymour
Welch, Leo D.
Welpton, Richard L.
Whalen, Grover
Whitaken, George A.
Whitaker, Samuel E.
White, Charles M.
Whitten, Jamie L.
Whittington, William M.
Wickard, Claude
Wideman, Frank J.
Willett, Wm. Edward
Williams, Albert N.
Williams, Aubrey
Williams, T. Morgan
Williman, Frank L.
Wilson, Lloyd B.
Windham, James C.
Wood, David F.
Woodfill, W. Stewart
Woodruff, Robert W.
Wozencraft, Frank W.
Wright, Warren
Wynn, William T.
Wynne, Jefferson

Young, Howard
Young, J. Russell

Ziskind, Jacob
Zukor, Adolf

Table of Contents

TABLE OF CONTENTS

x

PART ONE

CHAPTER 1

I Attract
an Autobiographer

Mine has been the kind of life that attracts autobiographers, but not biographers. To me it has been an extraordinary life, and I have long thought that somebody should write a book about it. And since I am the world's leading authority on the subject, I may as well do it myself. Then there is the further consideration that if I don't nobody else will.

Among the many reasons for the indifference of biographers to the material my life affords is the incontrovertible fact that I myself am not very remarkable by the vulgar standards of my times. Had I been President of the United States, biographers would be beating down my door. They would search through my personal papers, ferret out my secrets, disagree about the reasons for my mistakes, and tear me to pieces in a way that I myself have no intention of doing.

It is, all things considered, fortunate that I have never been President. It would be futile to deny that I have never been President, because the world is full of eccentric people who remember the names of past Presidents as well as other, more normal people remember the past performances of outstanding race horses. But I can say, in all honesty, that I have known some Presidents, the two most recent ones quite well, and that they, for better or for worse, have known me. In many ways, that is a more satisfactory situation all around. It leaves me in a position to describe these Presidents more impartially and to judge them more objectively than I could possibly describe and judge myself if I had been President. Moreover, it leaves the Presidents and their other associates free to deny any relationship with me.

Franklin D. Roosevelt and Harry S. Truman must be classified as Presidents of tremendous courage, if not always of infallible judgment. Both of them appointed me to jobs in their administrations.

Roosevelt made me a District of Columbia Commissioner, where I served with great distinction as one third of a mayor of Washington, and Truman appointed me to the Reconstruction Finance Corporation, where I served with equal éclat as one fifth of the directorate of the world's biggest bank.

Harry S. Truman is clearly my favorite, among the

Presidents I have known. He is also one of my favorite human beings, which is saying far more for him, because there are so many more people among my acquaintances who have not been President than people who have. He stands up well even in the larger field of competition. It isn't simple to see a President of the United States as he actually is. But Truman would be just as attractive if he were a county judge, as he once was. One of the most remarkable things about him is that the Presidency hasn't changed him.

I didn't know him when he was in Missouri, but I did know him when he was a freshman Senator and later when he was an unobtrusive Vice-President. How he became Vice-President is a story that I don't think has been fully told until now.

Before going any further, I should warn readers of this book that I mean to write primarily about me and only incidentally about Presidents and other famous people. Some of the people I shall be mentioning as I go along are infinitely more important than I am, but not to me. I shall drag in big names and significant places and events merely to dress up the show window in which I myself am the object most prominently exhibited. The background space I yield to others will be a grudging concession to the gross curiosity of the readers and to my own cupidity, neither of which I approve.

In other words, I shall try to include enough interesting material about the glamorous great to attract buyers to this book. I shall waste no time or words trying to seem

5

modest. I shall emulate Robert Tolman, an artist friend of mine, who once testified as an expert witness in a case involving the value of a picture. Under cross-examination, Tolman was asked who, in his opinion, was the world's greatest living portrait painter. "I am," he answered. Later a friend suggested to Tolman that his answer might seem immodest to some. "Perhaps," Tolman conceded. "But what could I do? I was under oath."

It is my observation, both of myself and of others, that every man is the center of his own universe. He is his own hero. As I go along, I shall contend, and undertake to prove, that I excelled all my contemporaries in some ways and am, therefore, unique.

At this point, I shall cite one example. Almost all the political experts, both professional and amateur, were wrong in their predictions about the outcome of the last Presidential election. But not one of them was more wrong than I. Indeed, I was even wronger than George Gallup.

To make it worse, I was, at the time of the campaign, a sort of self-appointed unofficial adviser to President Harry S. Truman. I was in a position to tell him how his campaign should be run, and I did so. All through the campaign Mr. Truman ignored my advice, and all through the campaign I kept promising myself that when he lost to Thomas E. Dewey I would remember to be generous and not say, "I told you so." When it was all over and he had won, I told him that I had been supremely confident of his defeat.

6

"So was everybody else," he confided, "but you're the first one who's admitted it."

My point is that whereas almost everybody was wrong on this occasion I managed to rise above the pack and get credit for being *outstandingly* wrong. I wasn't wrong in thinking that Harry Truman would be personally more attractive to the voters than Thomas E. Dewey; I knew he would be. But I had noted that people everywhere were demanding change and I remembered that the Democratic party had been in power sixteen years. I figured that the time had come when the people would want to clean out the courthouse. But what I failed to take into consideration was that the changes in government in England, Ireland, South Africa, and elsewhere had all been leftward changes. The people were tired of conservatives, not of liberals. In this country, the liberals were in, and a change would have brought conservatives to power. That wasn't what the voters here or in the rest of the world wanted at that time.

I have had many other successes in outstanding wrongness. Perhaps I should explain, in this connection, that immodesty is a family tradition with us Allens, and I feel duty bound to carry it on.

My uncle John M. Allen survived eight terms—sixteen years—in Congress during the Reconstruction period after the Civil War, in which he had served the Confederacy as a private soldier. He became nationally famous as "Private John Allen," and he made Tupelo, Mississippi, his home town, famous, too. *The Congressional*

Record shows that he started one speech with the announcement: "Mr. Chairman, I desire to say to those present that their perfect attention will not embarrass me in the least." And he ended it with this comment, after the Speaker had warned him that his time was up: "This is a pity, for I had many other things of great interest to say, but as my time has expired, and not wishing to further interrupt the proceedings, I will retire to the cloakroom to receive congratulations."

Even Uncle John's explanation for the start of the ill-advised War between the States was a boast about Tupelo. The story went this way. When the trouble started, Secretary of War Simon Cameron rushed into President Abraham Lincoln's office and shouted: "Mr. President, the South has seceded." Lincoln shrugged his shoulders and replied: "Well, let it secede." Cameron persisted: "But, Mr. President, Tupelo is in the South." That rocked Lincoln back on his heels, and he exclaimed: "My God! We can't give up Tupelo." And that was how the Civil War began.

This is my first expedition into the realm of belles-lettres and doubtless will be my last, since I have but one life to give to my countrymen. It is not easy. In my innocence, I had thought that an autobiography should start at the beginning, proceed at a leisurely pace up to the present, and then, perhaps, toss out a few sagacious opinions about the shape of the future. Not at all!

My literary advisers and publishers fully agreed that my autobiography should start at the present and work gradually back through my salad days to my fresh green youth, and should have very little of the salad and almost none of the youth. They insensitively estimated that readers wouldn't care to know about me, but only about my associates. I can scarcely credit this. But on the off-chance that my advisers are right, I suggest that my readers skip Part One, which has to do with my childhood and youth, and start with Part Two, which is mostly about others. Of course, doing it that way they will miss what I consider the best part of the story, but that, as my advisers point out, is their own business. I don't even object if they start with the last chapter and work forward. It will be easier for them to read that way than it would have been for me to write that way.

I shall probably live to regret writing this book, either forward or backward, because it is bound to become a more or less permanent record of my errors, but if I get into trouble, I shall remember the advice Sam Rosenman gave President Roosevelt in 1936. Campaigning for re-election that year, Roosevelt was confronted with the necessity of writing a speech to be delivered in Pittsburgh. Four years earlier, he had delivered a speech in the same place advocating drastic government economy. Now he wanted to advocate lavish government spending. It had occurred to him that some of his more unreasonable critics might find fault with this shift as a manifestation of inconsistency. What he wanted Rosenman to do was to figure out some way of executing this about-face and make it seem that Roosevelt was still marching in the same direction in 1936 as he had been in 1932. Rosenman thought it over for a few days and then told the President:

"I think, Mr. President, that I have found a way out."

"What is it, Sam?" Roosevelt eagerly asked.

"Deny that you made a speech in Pittsburgh in 1932."

CHAPTER 2

A Pity to Waste It
on the Young

LIKE all children, I was beset by fears, worries, and unreasonable adults. I believe it was George Bernard Shaw who observed that youth is so fine a thing it is a pity to waste it on the young. Only half of this statement is correct, in my opinion. I think it is a shame to have it at all.

Childhood is miserable for most people, and children, through no fault of their own, are an alien and hostile race who won't become tolerable until they grow up, if then. I find the theory of psychologists of the behaviorist school—that what we are going to be is determined by environment and by our reactions to it during the first few years of our lives—most depressing.

I don't like to think about my own youth, or anybody

else's, and I suspect that most middle-aged people who say they would like to live their childhoods over again don't really mean it. What they would like to do is to live them over again knowing what they know now, as adults in short pants. Myself, I wouldn't go through it again in any circumstances for anything. I'd rather be fat and fifty than than fifteen and foolish.

Yet I do have some pleasant memories about the small town I was brought up in, about my parents and their friends and the kind of life they led in those relatively simple, far-off, turn-of-the-century times.

My father and mother were Virginians, but not tidewater Virginians. They were from the hill country—of Scotch, Irish, and English stock—and the Allens they left behind in Virginia were still feuding among themselves after I was semigrown, much to my family's embarrassment. My part of the clan emigrated to Baldwyn, Mississippi, before I was born. Father, at the age of eleven, was a scout for General Forrest during the Civil War, and the first Allen home in Mississippi, now occupied by Judge Allen Cox, a relative of ours, still bears the plaque: "This house gave nine sons to the Confederacy." When one speaks of the war in that part of Mississippi, even now, it is the Civil War, unless otherwise designated. Nobody feels too happy about wars in which Southern boys have Yankee allies, as in the two World Wars. So it is only natural that the Allen home bears no plaque telling how many sons it has given—and there have been a good many —in other wars.

After the war, Father read law to prepare himself for practice in the courts of Mississippi. When he thought he was ready, he presented himself to a venerable jurist for the examination that, if he passed, would make him eligible. The judge who examined him, in announcing that he had made it, commented that he had shown "excellent moral qualifications and some knowledge of the law."

However little Father may have known about the law, he became a successful practitioner in Booneville, where he and one other lawyer, B. A. P. Selman, supplied the need for two counselors in every legal dispute. He sometimes took me to court with him to listen to the arguments. I think I remember one of his cases, but maybe I only remember what was told me about it later.

This case concerned the replevin of a cow, and it was tried in the courthouse around which Booneville grouped itself, by a justice of the peace who didn't like Father. Anyway, the decision went against Father's client, and Father protested vehemently, waving a volume of Blackstone under the justice's nose to emphasize his outrage.

"Sit down, Mr. Allen!" the judge shouted. "I know the law."

"Of course you do, Your Honor," Father replied. "I just wanted to read this to you to show you what a damned fool Blackstone was."

Father professed to be a pious man but of a sect that had no congregation in Booneville. The Methodist, Baptist, and Presbyterian churches, which flourished in our town, were too lax for him, he said. This being so, he was free to go fishing on Sunday. He was also free to go fishing on most weekdays. Fishing, he once explained to me, was his true profession, and the law was only a sideline. He sometimes took me with him, and once, when I got into trouble for playing hooky, wrote a note to my teacher saying, "George Ed wasn't in school today because he was fishing with me." That seemed an adequate excuse to him; it was always good enough to justify the postponement of a trial.

Father died when I was eight years old. Mother, an older sister, and a horde of kinfolk—uncles and aunts and cousins too numerous to catalogue—looked out for me after that. Mother was a shrewd business manager and managed what there was to manage well enough to supply us with all the necessities and many luxuries. My uncles were frugal Scots, mostly lawyers, and in the cotton business in one way or another. Uncle John was the clan's only political black sheep, and the family never quite knew whether to be very proud or a little ashamed of him. He soon became my favorite and my idol; nothing was so much fun as going with him to speakings, not even revival meetings, where in my early youth I was frequently converted and reconverted to Methodist Christianity.

One of the luxuries Mother supplied while I was still quite young was a pony on which I played cowboy. One day while I was galloping after imaginary horse rustlers over the field of our neighbor, Doc Fulgum, I swung my lariat and, much to my amazement, successfully lassoed his colt. My pony and I were so excited that we jerked in unison and broke the colt's neck. On that occasion I emulated Parson Weems' George Washington; I told Doc Fulgum what had happened. He praised my honesty, my mother praised my honesty; and I became so enamored of honesty that I got into all sorts of troubles before I finally concluded that honesty was a virtue that could be overdone, particularly when carried to the lengths of making up bad stories about oneself in order to bask in the sense of virtue that comes from making a clean breast of an imaginary peccadillo. Mother, for all her indulgence, caught on to that pretty fast.

After what we always referred to as the "accident" with the pony, my maternal grandfather, Plaxico, who had done well lending money to cotton planters at the going rate of ten per cent interest, was requested to sell the pony. He got sixty dollars for it but didn't give me the money. Instead, he loaned it out through his private bank and a year later gave me the six dollars it had earned to feel and play with. Then the six dollars was taken back and loaned out along with the sixty dollars. The next year I was permitted to handle the interest on sixty-six dollars. Grandfather thus taught me the lesson in thrift that I have spent the rest of my life ignoring. Or it may be that I did learn a lesson, but not the lesson Grandfather intended to teach. I learned that money wasn't good for anything except spending—that as a plaything in itself it was about as satisfactory as spinach.

As soon as I was deemed old enough to leave home, I was packed off to McTyeire Preparatory School in McKenzie, Tennessee, to be stuffed with education. But I resisted the stuffing process stubbornly and, I must say in justice to myself, rather successfully. James Robins, later professor of Latin at Vanderbilt, now emeritus, who was head of McTyeire in my time, apparently thought he could build my character even if he couldn't stuff my mind, and I must concede that his private lectures sometimes impressed me. Just before the summer vacation he gave me such a convincing talk on the character-building properties of hard labor that I got a job plowing. After the first day of it, I went home with a nosebleed and Mother immediately decided that I was too frail for that kind of character building. I agreed with her after a decent show of protest. The rest of that summer was spent in delightful indolence at Colorado Springs, Colorado.

Years later, Professor Robins turned up at Cumberland University to see me awarded an honorary degree. He congratulated me warmly and told me frankly that of all the boys who had ever gone to McTyeire, I had seemed to him least likely ever to achieve a degree of any description.

Having tried hard labor and found that I wasn't suited to it, I did experiment with other kinds of work to supply myself with soda money. One of my positions was with Western Union. One day a message came through to the Booneville telegraph office notifying a citizen that the corpse of one of his relatives was arriving that day on the afternoon train. On the way to deliver the message I was interested by some old friends in a catfishing enterprise that wasn't expected to take very long and became so absorbed in it that I forgot all about the prior errand. It was a very hot day, and the consequence of my negligence became apparent before the next morning when I reported for work. To state the outcome as gracefully as possible, I can report that there was no insistent demand on the part of Western Union for my continued services to that company. Years later, when functioning as an RFC official, and a Western Union loan application came to me for decision, I tried hard to be objective, but Western Union didn't get all it wanted. Incidentally, railroads now insist that corpses be accompanied by live escorts. The railroads owe me something for my catfishing because that incident helped them establish the rule under which they now collect fares for two instead of one when they undertake a mission of this kind.

I was not greatly concerned about my dismissal from Western Union, because I had excellent soda prospects at the time that were not dependent on my own efforts. My sister, who was almost ten years my senior, was being courted by one of the town's two druggists and one of the town's two bankers. The druggist, who operated the most enticing clubhouse and soda dispensary in Booneville, was a glamorous figure to me and, I therefore assumed, to my sister also. The banker, on the other hand, was just another banker. To my utter amazement and complete disgust, she married the banker, and I held it against her for years.

My first real political experience was gained in 1912 at the Baltimore Democratic Convention. L. M. Phillips, the Booneville delegate, found that he could not attend but that he could appoint an alternate, and I persuaded him to appoint me. I was sixteen years old. The trip to Baltimore was an experience in itself; it was the first time I'd ever ventured that far from home. I marched and shouted for Oscar W. Underwood and never did quite understand how he lost the nomination to Woodrow Wilson. To my schoolboy mind the defeat of Underwood was an injury and the victory of a schoolteacher was an almost unbearable added insult.

Having been told that travel broadened one, I determined to make the most of my opportunity, exhausted as my services to Underwood had left me, and so went on to New York when the Convention was over. I had dreamed for years of seeing the fabulous sights of America's greatest city. Arriving in New York, where I could remain only a day and a night, I put up at the old Breslin Hotel on Twenty-eighth Street, lay down in my room for a nap, and woke up twenty-one hours later, just in time to catch my train back to Mississippi.

And that's about all I remember, or, at least, want to remember, about my youth in Booneville.

CHAPTER 3

No Mood
to Dicker

EDUCATION is a fine thing and doubtless deserves the high reputation it enjoys, particularly with the uneducated. Like everything else, it is valued more highly by those who don't have it than by those who do. Being well schooled, but not, I should say, well educated, I am in a position to be realistic about it. I think enough of it to want my nephews and nieces to go to the best colleges and make high grades, but not enough of it to clutter my own mind with a lot of useless information. I know quite a few people who are educated beyond their intelligence, but some of the best educated people I know didn't go to the best colleges, or, indeed, to any colleges at all. Still, it is my firm opinion that all bright boys and girls should be exposed to education so they can catch it if they are not immune.

As between various systems of higher education, here and abroad, I have no very firm opinions. But I happen to know that President Truman does. The question came up at the White House shortly after the Congressional election of 1946, which gave the Republicans control of both the House and the Senate. Among the American statesmen who worried out loud about how a Democratic President was going to get along with a Republican Congress was Senator J. William Fulbright, an extremely able Arkansas Democrat. Fulbright advocated that Truman resign after appointing a Republican Secretary of State, who would then succeed him (since there was no Vice-President at the time)—this giving the GOP complete responsibility for running the government until the Presidential election of 1948 gave the people a chance to elect a new Congress and a new President of their own choice.

Having studied in England as a Rhodes scholar, Fulbright doubtless came to admire the British parliamentary system so much that he couldn't quite see how a President chosen by one party and a Congress representing the other, antipathetical as the parties were, would manage to get the country through the critical postwar years. But Truman, who knew the American system thoroughly and thought there was nothing as good anywhere on earth, took a quite different view. Commenting on

Fulbright's proposal, he said: "What this country needs is more land-grant colleges."

I attended several of the colleges in the South, but left them flat after giving them a fair try, sometimes at their suggestion and sometimes at my own, before settling down to sweat out a law degree and, even more important, to learn enough law to pass a state board. My diploma has been so little used that it is almost as good as new.

The process of getting my degree was so painful that I cannot bring myself to dwell upon it here. My principal interest in college was athletics, though even in my college days I was primarily a spectator sportsman. I have always liked to watch games of almost any kind, particularly rough games like football, where other fellows bruise each other. I can get all the exercise I want for myself—and enough bruises—climbing to my seat in the stands. And I get as much fun out of watching horses beat each other as watching men doing the same thing. I have always felt that fishing is a good excuse for sitting in a boat, but otherwise not very thrilling. I don't get much satisfaction out of outthinking and outfighting a fish.

As for the mammals, I have no trouble feeling superior to the rabbit without shooting him, but, though I have never gone big-game hunting, I have a notion that I might not be so cocky in the same acre of woods with a panther or in the same ring with a bull; I am content to leave it to fellows like Ernest Hemingway to wave humanity's banner in these arenas.

It has always seemed to me that the great Senator John Randolph of Roanoke, Virginia, spoke well on this subject. Randolph never managed to grow any whiskers and spoke in a high, squeaky voice but out of a brilliant mind. One colleague was so incautious as to refer in an oblique and taunting way to these deficiencies of Randolph's. Replying, the gentleman from Virginia said he would not undertake to compete with the distinguished Senator in an area where "every jackass is infinitely his superior."

My athletic prowess in college days was devoted principally to semipro baseball. It was the standard dream of every boy in our part of the country to make the Memphis baseball team of the Southern League. Training for this destiny, which was never fulfilled, I played with a lot of Southern bush-league clubs. The game I remember best was one I played in between Iuka (Mississippi) and Tuscumbia (Alabama). It was an epic of baseball history and deserves to be a part of this immortal chronicle.

I was playing in the outfield for Iuka. My team was ahead 1 to 0 in the last half of the ninth inning, with two men out and two strikes on the batter but with a dangerous Tuscumbia base runner on third. The Iuka pitcher was weakening and our catcher's arm was beginning to give out, too, so he wanted to end the game without an extra-inning tussle, which Iuka was ill prepared to face. The catcher decided upon a desperate stratagem. After every pitched ball up to the count of two strikes and two balls, he pegged to third. After the third ball, he threw wild. The runner steamed home, only to be tagged out at the plate. What our catcher had thrown wild was a peeled potato. What happened then is now called a "rhubarb," but this "rhubarb" was a brawl that neither Iuka nor Tuscumbia will ever forget. This incident caused a change in the rules of the great American game. Ever since, it has been illegal to use more than one ball at a time, real or phony.

President Robert Hutchins of the University of Chicago was years behind the authorities of Cumberland in his decision to banish football. In 1916, either because they thought the sport was being overemphasized or because Cumberland couldn't afford the kind of talent it would need to compete successfully in its class, the powers that were decided against football. My youthful spirits were so outraged by this decision that I determined, if possible, to overrule it. The chance came when John W. Heisman, then the coach of Georgia Tech, proposed a Cumberland-Tech game at Atlanta. In my capacity as manager I accepted the challenge on behalf of Cumberland and proceeded to get up a team, which I did by adding a few ringers to the Cumberland roster. After some secret practice sessions, my Cumberland irregulars looked pretty hot to me, and I went to Atlanta on the big day full of high hopes for an upset.

But my team (I appointed myself Captain) somehow couldn't get rolling on the offensive or stop rolling on the defensive. Before it was over I had to leave the security of the bench, from which I had been guiding Cumberland's strategy, and go in at fullback myself. John Nelson, now manager of the Hot Springs, Arkansas, Chamber of Commerce, who was one of my ringers, testifies to the intrepidity of my play. He says he was skirting end on one play with me behind him, that he fumbled and shouted to me to fall on the ball, whereupon I shouted back, "Fall on it yourself. You dropped it." I believe this story to be apocryphal. There are, however, certain statistics hidden away in football archives that might be interesting to the kind of stuffy people who concern themselves with statistics. Score—Georgia Tech, 222; Cumberland, o. (One of the largest scores in the history of football.) This game also set three more records: (1) greatest number of points after touchdown; (2) greatest number of touchdowns from kickoff; (3) greatest number of yards gained.

I am sure the score would have been even bigger had we not stopped receiving and begun kicking off after touchdowns. That system, on the occasions when the kicks were not blocked, forced them to run the whole distance of the field for the next touchdown instead of from the place where we fumbled. We played five more games that season and never penetrated our opponents' side of the field.

My good friend, Chip Robert, whom I later succeeded as Secretary of the Democratic National Committee, was Graduate Manager of Athletics at Georgia Tech in 1916. The assistant coach was John Brookes, a distinguished lawyer, with whom I now serve on the Republic Steel Board. John is always exaggerating, claiming that we were defeated by the ridiculous score of 232 to o.

24

Grantland Rice, in ending his story of the game, stated that the greatest individual play made by Cumberland occurred when Fullback Allen circled right end for a six-yard loss. That ended my football career.

Having finished Cumberland second from last in a class of 178 (my feeling of inferiority to that fellow persists to this day: how could he have estimated what one could get away with more accurately than I?), I hung out my shingle in Okolona, Chickasaw County, Mississippi, near Uncle John's town of Tupelo. Uncle John had made this region the seat of a famous Federal fish hatchery. Speaking in the House of Representatives on behalf of an appropriation for the hatchery, he had insisted with such eloquence that the fish themselves favored Tupelo that Congress could not resist his pleas. Uncle John had ended his argument with, "Gentlemen, there are thousands of unborn fish waiting to be born in Tupelo." There, I became George E. Allen, Counselor at Law, with the firm intention of growing up with Uncle John's fish in one of the biggest little towns in the South. Okolona's population was 1500, though the Chamber of Commerce claimed 2000.

I established myself snugly on the top floor of the Merchants Bank and Trust Building, and just across from me, also on the second floor, was Dr. Rutledge, a forward-looking dentist. Our relationship was mutually beneficial. He was experimenting with the use of gas and often needed a witness to swear he hadn't used too much of it, just in case one of his patients shouldn't wake up, through no fault of his own. In return, he stood ready to be my witness in any case that might come along. That didn't place much burden on him.

Along about April, 1917, I successfully settled my first important lawsuit. It involved injury to a lady who had tripped over an umbrella strapped to a suitcase and protruding into the aisle of a day coach on the Mobile and Ohio Railroad, running from Mobile, Alabama, to St. Louis, Missouri. My client had suffered painful injuries and serious embarrassments and was entitled to the $40,000 damages for which I filed claim.

After several conferences with A. T. Stovall, Chickasaw County's most distinguished corporation lawyer, in which he brazenly contended that I had no case, I settled for ten dollars, of which I got five dollars and my client five dollars. I was in no mood to dicker.

One of the pleasantest, if least celebrated, Okolona institutions at the time I took up residence there was the poker game that went on almost nightly over the R. B. Smith grocery store. I occasionally found time to relax from the rigors of my law practice by participating in this game. Two other regular participants were Horton Robinson, the druggist, and Ed Wynn, a cotton buyer. One night, as the first gray streaks of dawn started creeping up over the horizon at the end of Main Street, both of them were dealt extraordinary hands. But they hadn't fared very well earlier in the night and both of them were finding it a simple matter to see over the piles of chips at their places at the table. After a little betting and raising, Ed suggested to Horton: "Let's take these hands, seal them in envelopes, go out and raise a little more money, and then come back and bet some more." Horton, allowing that he had a whale of a hand himself, said the plan appealed to him. So Horton washed his face, ate breakfast at the Mobile and Ohio Depot lunch stand, and then went to the First National Bank to negotiate a loan with the president, Mr. Tom A. O'Hara.

O'Hara had not yet arrived, but a smart young fellow from St. Louis, the new cashier, consented to interview Horton, who proposed a $2000 loan. What collateral? "A jack-high straight flush," said Horton, explaining the circumstances. "Ridiculous," said the new cashier, "I've never heard of such a preposterous suggestion." So Horton went away empty-handed.

When O'Hara arrived at the bank, the cashier informed him, overflowing with righteousness and obviously expecting to be commended, of what he had done. There was a long silence before O'Hara spoke. Finally he said, "Horton is quite a poker player. What did he say he had?" The young man replied, "Well, he said he had a jack-high straight flush, but did you ever hear of anything so ridiculous?" Mr. O'Hara interrupted him with, "A jack-high straight flush? Listen, young man, as long as I am president of this bank, a jack-high straight flush will be good for the total assets of this institution."

My promising career in Okolona was interrupted before it was well begun by the declaration of war on Germany. Obviously, I would go to war. The question was how. I consulted Uncle John, who had made a national reputation as "Private John" and whose political stock in trade had been his boast that he had never even got a corporal's stripes out of his service to the Confederacy. At political meetings he liked to say, particularly when running against a former officer, "Now, all of you who were generals vote for my opponent, and all who were common soldiers, like me, vote for Private John Allen."

I went over to near-by Tupelo to consult Uncle John. To my surprise, he advised me to get a commission, if possible. His argument was that there had been enough privates in the Allen family—that for another to be a private would be showing off too much and a general or two wouldn't do our prestige any harm. Accordingly, I made a deal with Spec Hairston, then the Mississippi Adjutant General, to raise a company of militia and get, as a reward, a first lieutenancy.

He got my commission by Governor Theodore G. Bilbo, somewhat to my surprise, because the Allens and the Bilbos were implacable political enemies. The reason Bilbo gave for signing my commission was that he wanted to give me a chance to die for the cause of democracy, on the theory that Mississippi would be better off if the Allen clan were exterminated. I don't think he meant it. That was merely his way of exchanging pleasantries with Uncle John, who never mentioned Bilbo's name before ladies. He said it was vulgar.

Uncle John's attitude toward Bilbo has always seemed to me like that of a certain Miss Beulah Jones toward her friend Leonard Smith. Beulah once turned up at Columbia Hospital, a Washington institution that specializes in maternity cases. Although at Columbia for the usual reason, Beulah made a point of insisting that she was unmarried.

"That's a bit unusual," said the clerk who interviewed her. "What's the father's name?"

"Smith—Leonard Smith," Miss Jones replied.

She was admitted, and her baby was born in due course, no further questions asked. And in about a year she was back.

"Well, Beulah," said the same clerk, "back again. I suppose you're married now."

"No, not yet," said Beulah.

"Who's the father this time?"

"Leonard Smith."

Another year went by, and the same thing happened again.

"Why in the world don't you marry him?" the clerk asked this time.

"Well," said Beulah, "he just doesn't appeal to me."

Uncle John had once made the rash promise that he'd leave Mississippi if Bilbo was re-elected Governor. When he was re-elected, Bilbo sent Uncle John a wire reminding him of his promise and received this answer: "Mississippi has gone to hell and I'm going to St. Louis." Uncle John came back to Mississippi, but never again acknowledged that he was a Mississippian. He always signed himself: "Private John Allen, Tupelo, U.S.A."

Bilbo's signature wasn't all I needed to be an officer; unfortunately, I had to satisfy a regular army board, which was so important that it used eagle colonels for orderlies, that I was qualified to lead American soldiers. This board decided that I and lots of other national-guard officers lacked every qualification except political influence. But I told the board how important this war was to me, how I had left home only three weeks before with the town band out to play martial music for the departing hero, and it let me keep my commission.

I fought the good fight in triplicate at Camp Beauregard, Louisiana, through the early months of the war and then was sent to France, where I never heard a gun fired in anger. It probably wasn't an accident that I was one of the first officers sent home after the Armistice, when General Pershing was deciding what help he could dispense with most easily. Unlike most of the First World War officers I have known, I wasn't in line for promotion when the war ended.

But I was pleased, after I got home, to receive a letter from President Wilson asking me to retain my first lieutenant's commission in the reserve corps. This invitation was later repeated by Presidents Harding, Coolidge, and Hoover, and when, at last, President Roosevelt was elected I complained to my friend, Senator Pat Harrison, about my rank. By that time, I figured, I was the oldest first lieutenant in the nation. Now that we Democrats were back in power, I contended, I had a right to expect a captaincy. Harrison agreed that deserving Democrats should get some deserved promotions. Accordingly, he sent a letter of protest to the army on my behalf, and I promptly received a letter notifying me that my name had been dropped from the reserve rolls. Instead of promoting me, the army had fired me. Harrison fully agreed with me that that was a hell of a way to run an army, but there wasn't anything to do about it except complain, which we did.

About the only thing I have ever resented about my army service was the case of olives I had to pay for when I left Camp Beauregard. I had been in charge of the officers' mess, and a wholesale grocer from Alexandria, Louisiana, was at the train to collect for those olives when I left the place—said they never had been paid for. I paid for them out of my own pocket with some reluctance and under duress, and have spent the rest of my life trying to get even by eating an extra olive at every dinner and banquet I attend.

After the war I returned to Okolona, but somehow it didn't seem such a big little town as I remembered it. I had discovered that there was a world beyond the boundaries of Mississippi and even beyond the Mason-Dixon line and presently, for better or worse, I made my way into it, fully educated, as my college diploma attested, and a man of the world, as my discharge papers bore witness. Thus equipped, I ventured fearlessly into the wilds of far-off Indiana, accepting in perfectly good faith and with too much innocence Horace Greeley's advice to go west.

CHAPTER 4

The One
Not Present

WHAT helped me make up my mind to leave Okolona was
a courtroom incident that had cruelly stabbed my professional pride. I happened to be in court during the ar-
raignment of a young colored man accused of house-
breaking. The judge had explained to him that he was
entitled to the services of a defense attorney—that the
attorneys available to him were Bob Cook, George Bean,
or George Allen, we being the only three young trial lawyers in town. The judge had asked the three of us to stand
up. Bean and I did so, but Cook wasn't in the courtroom
and a bailiff so informed the judge.

"Well, here are Mr. Allen and Mr. Bean," the judge

told the prisoner. "You may have your choice, one of these or the one not present."

"Judge, I believe I'll take the one not present," said the defendant.

It was fortunate, therefore, that at about this time I received a wire from an old college friend named Bruce, informing me that he had opened a law office in Greensburg, Indiana, that he was doing splendidly and needed a partner. Since my law practice wasn't much and Greensburg had the virtue of being a faraway place, I decided to be Bruce's partner sight unseen. Okolona, I said to myself, had known me as a fuzzy-cheeked youth and would have a hard time getting used to the idea that I was now twenty-two and a barrister of great acumen.

It got back to me at about this time that an older member of the Okolona bar was saying that young George Allen gave promise of abolishing lynching in our county. "Get George to defend him," this smart aleck had explained, "and we can hang anybody we want to—legally." I decided to go to a newer, cleaner, friendlier land, out where the Western frontier was closer and opportunity bigger.

I was a little crestfallen to find that Bruce's law practice was, in fact, a collection agency and nothing to challenge a man of my attainments. But I had read in the *Indianapolis Star* on the way to Greensburg that the Governor of Indiana had just appointed one of the partners in the town's leading law firm, Davidson and Craig, a state judge. So I called on the remaining partner, Tom

Davidson, then President of the Indiana Bar Association, and informed him that I was prepared to take Mr. Craig's place in the firm. He was amused rather than outraged by this brashness and said he'd let me have Judge Craig's office, though not his partnership, if I were prepared to settle down in a practice that would net me from seven to eight dollars a week. Since my room at the YMCA cost only two dollars a week, the pay was adequate.

Mr. Davidson had a summer place at Eagle River, Wisconsin, and went there with his family the following summer, leaving me to handle his affairs. Handling his affairs was a matter of asking for a continuance every time one of his cases came up in court. I did this, if I do say so, rather brilliantly. I did it so well, in fact, that I was permitted that fall to assist Mr. Davidson in the presentation before an Interstate Commerce Commission examiner of a rate case involving what we contended was discrimination against Indiana in favor of Illinois shippers. I mention this case not because of its intrinsic fascination, but because it changed the course of my life.

I admit with some embarrassment that I had found, when I got to Indiana, that my Mississippi accent was unusual enough to seem strange, and, to some, amusing. Like thousands of professional Southerners before and since, I made the most of it. My accent got so thick my own people in Mississippi couldn't have understood me. One of the Hoosiers who thought my appeal in the rate case excruciatingly droll was A. W. McCain, then managing director of the Indiana State Chamber of Commerce.

He dazzled me with an offer of seventy-five dollars a week
—not a month or a year—to work for the Chamber, the
work to consist principally of delivering entertaining
talks to local units and otherwise making myself useful. I
made after-dinner speeches in darkest Mississippi you-all
dialect to people whose normal speech would have
sounded like dialect in Mississippi.

From Indianapolis, where I lived while working for
the Indiana Chamber of Commerce, I went to Louisville,
Kentucky, to drum up convention business as a director
of the Louisville Convention and Publicity League. I was
a convention lurer. I went around the country telling or-
ganizations about the attractions of Louisville as a convention locale. Later I did the same thing for West Baden
and French Lick, Indiana resorts, the latter owned by
Tom Taggart, one of the old wheelhorses of the Democratic party. There I met Albert W. Hawkes of the General Chemical Company, later U. S. Senator for New Jersey, who told me New York needed me, which I thought
very knowing of New York, so I went there with him. He
gave me a payroll number and a desk but no duties before taking himself off for Europe. For several months
nobody paid any attention to me and all I did was collect
my salary. I liked the salary part of it and the inactivity,
but I couldn't stand the isolation, so I told Hawkes, when
he got home, that General Chemical and New York would
have to get along as best they could without me.

Hawkes gave me an argument. He said he'd bought
into a gadget to regulate automobile traffic by flashing

stop-and-go signs alternately at street intersections. I tried to be as kind as I could about it. I patiently explained to Hawkes that I had been brought up in a political family and knew the ways of politics and politicians. This device of his, I pointed out, would cut down the number of police needed in cities, that in cutting down the number of police needed it would reduce the patronage of the party in power and that any politician who had achieved the eminence of a place on a city council would cut his own throat before he'd hand over to a machine a job his uncle Charlie on his mother's side could fill just as well, if not better. Hawkes, who probably made a fortune out of his interest in stop-and-go signals, was satisfyingly depressed by my refusal, out of political sophistication, to believe that there was any future in automatic traffic cops.

Every crossroads in the land now has a traffic light—even Bud Maytag's town in Alabama. Maytag tells the story of one of his plantation hands driving slowly through the red light after waiting for the green to change when the signal was first installed. When the sheriff pounced upon him, Bud's man explained: "I saw this contraption here and I saw all you white folks going through on the green light and I figured the red light was for us colored folks to go through."

I was still wondering at Hawkes' naïveté when I ran into an old army friend of mine who owned a new process for making sugar sirup but needed capital. I didn't have much capital, but I'd saved a little, and I assured him that I could get more. My way of getting more was to run a "capital wanted" ad in a newspaper. This ad produced a man named Mac Tyge, one of the best dressed, most charming, most correct men it will ever be my ill fortune to know. He graciously permitted my partner and me to wine and dine him nightly in New York's most exclusive clubs. He assured us that our financial worries were over. Details of our business with him were to be taken up later with his lawyer, former Ambassador James W. Gerard. One day my partner and I discovered that Mac Tyge was mysteriously missing, along with the $50,000 we had put into our sirup venture; the next day we learned that Gerard had never heard of him but that the police had. He was the kind of salesman who could have sold double-breasted suits to Phi Beta Kappas.

It was at this low moment that I got a wire from H. L. Kaufman, president of the Congress Hotel in Chicago, offering me a job. A year or so earlier I had tried to sell him a plan for co-operative hotel promotion. He hadn't been interested in the plan, but he had then made me the offer he was now repeating. I grabbed it and for the next two years, in Chicago, I had a chance to fulfill my boyhood yearning to run one of the places where traveling men and other strangers live.

It is probably so that there's no business like show business, but the thing that comes closest is hotel business. The hotels I knew in the small Southern towns where I lived as a boy and young man were centers of cosmopolitanism, also culture. People from over the horizon, from places as far off as New York City, came to them and enriched their public rooms with worldly lore. These visitors were principally drummers—traveling men, we called them. They were gay, witty, and, one suspected, rather naughty fellows. The best people didn't like to have their daughters go out with traveling men, but the best fathers liked to talk with them in the hotel lobbies. They were bards and storytellers as well as salesmen. I suppose some of them were as tragic figures as the hero in *Death of a Salesman,* but we to whom they brought goods and tidings from the outside world didn't suspect it.

Hotel managers and clerks were glamorous in our towns because some of the sheen of the strangers from over the hills rubbed off on them. But they tended to be cynical—or, perhaps, merely realistic. In Tupelo there were two hotels and the clerk in one of them was an elderly wise man named "Pop" Carlton. A breezy young traveling man representing one of the big Chicago packing houses one day inquired of Pop's health and got the answer: "Not so good. Someday you're going to come in here and find a new face behind this desk."

"Look, Pop," said that packer's man, "if that ever happens we won't be coming here. You're the only reason we don't go to the other hotel."

"That's just pretty talk," said Pop. "When you find somebody else behind this desk, you'll say, 'Where's Pop?' and you'll be told, 'Pop's dead, hadn't you heard?' And you'll say, 'Poor old guy. What time's supper?' "

Pop used to tell the story, swearing it was true, about the inebriate who came in to register and noticed, just as he was doing so, a beetle that looked remarkably like a bedbug crawling across the desk. "I have been in a lot of hotels," said the guest, "and I've been attacked often by smart hotel bedbugs, but this is the first time a bedbug has ever come down to see what room I was going to get."

I was attracted to the hotel business as some are attracted by the theater. A hotel, to me, was a temporary haven for transients, and transients were always a potential adventure because, among many of them, one might happen upon a good talker, or, even better, a good listener. Talking has always been my favorite pastime. I play bridge and golf and, I sometimes think, engage in politics and business principally to have an excuse to talk with others who are more seriously following these pursuits. Useless play and work can sometimes be interrupted, if one is on the scene, for a little important talk. I have often thought that my system in college of staying alert at all the midnight bull sessions and sleeping in class had its advantages as a way of acquiring useful knowledge.

I soon learned that hotel business is fairly simple. Supply the hotel, and the customers will tell you exactly how to run it. As Bemelmans has demonstrated, no group in the world is so irrational as hotel customers unless it is hotel employees. At the Congress, we had a house detective who, in a spirit of friendly co-operation, once helped two robbers remove a grand piano from the mezzanine floor to a waiting truck. This same Sam Spade was quite capable of raiding the room of a married octogenarian couple and demanding to see their wedding license.

At the Congress I once found a Gideon Bible containing a thoughtful marginal note. It was one of the Bibles that told guests in a pasted-in foreword what chapters were recommended for despondency, loneliness, and other such maladies afflicting the spirit of the weary traveler. For loneliness, the recommended cure was Psalm 23. This particular Bible bore a note in a neat feminine handwriting at the end of Psalm 23. It said: "If still lonely, call Greenwich 2384."

By this time, the twenties were roaring around me; new-era prosperity was making millionaires of us all. I naturally drifted into hotel finance. Hugh McLennon, a North Side real-estate operator, was making a great success of the Lake Shore Drive Hotel, which Queen Marie of Romania had helped publicize, and I wanted to meet him. I arranged it by pretending that I was interested in buying the Belmont Hotel, another North Side property of his that wasn't doing so well. I, of course, didn't buy the Belmont, but I did become a partner of McLennon in several other ventures. I also associated myself with Richard Lane, president of the Blackhawk Hotels of Iowa, and his brother, J. Reed Lane. With the Lanes we bought the Ambassador Hotel in Kansas City for $10,000 cash and lots of notes and later the Grove Park Inn in Asheville, North Carolina, for an equally unbelievable sum. The financial fantasy of the times was such that we made a net profit of $90,000 the first month we operated the Grove Park Inn. On paper—and paper the banks were willing to take seriously, to my everlasting amazement—

I suddenly became rich. Fortunately, as it turned out later, I was somewhat more realistic about my status than the banks were. When the crash came, I hadn't spent the money I never had.

In the course of my operations with the Lanes, I met Harry L. Stuart, president of Halsey, Stuart and Company, one of the truly great American financiers, for the past several years the biggest investment banker in the world. Stuart had loaned about $13,000,000 to Harry Wardman, the Washington builder, who was getting into very deep water financially, and sent the Lane brothers and me to Washington to take over the Wardman properties. So, in 1929, I swanked into Washington in a chauffeur-driven town car and prepared to settle down to the joys of high living among the great in the seat of American government.

Things didn't work out quite as I had intended, principally because I woke up one fine morning to find myself more than $500,000 in debt. Of course, it was no distinction to be in the red for a half million. Some of my friends boasted financial failures running into the millions. Mine wasn't even big enough to make good dinner conversation, in those times.

What had happened to me was that I had pyramided a relatively small cash investment in Midwestern hotels into a piece of a big hotel empire. The syndicate in which I participated controlled more than twenty hotels, some of them big ones. Small down payments, subject to bonds, debentures, and preferred stocks, gave us control.

Unpyramiding after the depression hit turned out to be a lot harder than the pyramiding had been. At one time I was advised by a Washington banker to bail myself out by going through bankruptcy. But I demurred at this, attractive as it appeared at the time. I finally got myself in the clear by borrowing on my life insurance to pay off part of my debt, by negotiating part-payment compromises with some of my bankers and with bond-holders' protective committees, and by sacrificing all my collateral and equities.

Broke as I was, Washington was my meat and my milieu. It was a place where people liked to talk and seemed to have time for it. It was the place of all places for an amateur politician like me to kibitz on the professionals. Since then I have made a pleasant career of it. I still live at the Wardman Park Hotel, but now I'm one of the eccentric customers instead of one of the eccentric operators. This way I have more to say about how it is run.

PART TWO

CHAPTER 5

I Want It Expunged
from the Record

WASHINGTON in 1929 was still an overgrown American country town dangling in limbo between North and South, between metropolitan urbanity and rural parochialism, between the nineteenth and the twentieth centuries. The pace of life was a slow trot. Everybody had leisure for bridge and golf; so, naturally, Bobby Jones and Ely Culbertson made almost as many headlines as Herbert Hoover and Charles Curtis. The only real excitement was provided by a social war between Dolly Gann and Alice Roosevelt Longworth over the question: should the Speaker's lady sit higher at table than the Vice-President's lady, or vice versa? Even this fight probably wouldn't have created much excitement except that the redoubtable Mrs. Eleanor "Cissie" Patterson allied herself with Mrs. Gann and evened things up by attacking Mrs. Longworth's exposed salad flank.

Having been less excited than the rest of the country about the stock-market skyrocket, Washington was also less agitated about indications that the ball of fire had reached its apex and was about to fall to earth in fiery bits. For quite a while, in fact, President Herbert Hoover and his advisers simply refused to recognize that the ball wasn't going to keep right on defying gravity. Washington's reflexes were so slow that it was just getting ready for a real-estate boom of its own as the boom era was ending for the rest of the country. My idea in going to Washington was to ride that belated boom. I rode it, all right, but not in the direction intended. I had expected to feel the wind in my hair, but it hit me elsewhere.

The Republican party was, of course, in full command of the capital. The only Democrats around were from the Solid South, and all they did was harass the Administration in a halfhearted fashion. Nothing divided the two parties except the traditional disagreement over tariffs, and even this had become a phony issue to all except a few leftover free-traders like Cordell Hull of Tennessee. Most Democrats had become reconciled to high tariffs; they were perfectly willing to accept tariffs on the products of their own states as long as they were free to attack tariffs on the products of other states. To be sure, a few eccentric troublemakers like Robert F. Wagner of New York were muttering about unemployment—poverty in

46

the midst of plenty, they called it—but nobody paid much attention to them. What we were entering, according to Republicans and to most right-minded Democrats as well, was an era of perpetual prosperity to be sustained by a constantly rising standard of living exemplified by two cars in every garage.

I reveal no confidential information in stating that the smash came in October. I had installed myself in a suite at the Wardman Park Hotel overlooking sightly Rock Creek Valley. My imposing motorcar could be—and frequently was—summoned to take me to golf courses or bridge tables or elsewhere. The car so impressed one of the attractive young ladies who lived near the Wardman Park that she was induced, the following year, to become Mrs. Allen. She says now that it was the only town car ever seen on her street and, naturally, irresistibly alluring.

After that fateful October the Wardman Park emptied so fast you would have thought it was about to be quarantined for smallpox. Soon I was almost alone. The Lane brothers and I had taken over the hotel and other properties at the instigation of Harry Stuart, and presently we organized a bondholders' protective committee on which Joseph Tumulty, former secretary of President Wilson, Thomas Carson, representing a banking group, and Julius Peyser, a Washington banker, consented to serve. All the bondholders were completely bailed out, thanks to the astute management of Stuart, despite the constant cries of the Washington press that the investors were being gypped.

This whole operation was later investigated by the Senate Pecora Committee, which found nothing extraordinary in it. On the day that he was to appear before Pecora for the first time, Stuart's family was, of course, concerned, particularly his eighty-year-old father. One of Stuart's sisters overheard the elder Stuart that day invoking Divine protection on behalf of his son. He was specific: "Oh Lord," he said, "protect my son, Harry Stuart, president of Halsey, Stuart and Company, who is being persecuted by the Senate Banking and Currency Committee, in Washington—Washington, D. C., that is, Senate Office Building, Room 304."

One of the few guests who remained in residence at the Wardman Park, and continued to pay his bills regularly, fully realized how important he was to us, and his domineering behavior toward the employees showed it. One day I received an alarmed summons from an assistant manager, who said something dreadful had happened at the front door. I rushed down to find that our paying guest had been shot by the colored doorman, who still held the gun in his hand and was muttering to himself when I got there. I loaded him in my car and headed for the nearest police station. The doorman didn't object. On the contrary, he was more than willing to pay whatever price society would charge for his crime. Answering my question as to why he had done such a thing, he explained: "Mr. Allen, I just didn't like his attitude."

My prosperity and the nation's ended simultaneously. And the event had somewhat the same effect on me as on the country. Instead of thinking of Wall Street and La Salle Street as the power centers of American life, I began to think of the White House and the Capitol as its mainsprings. Until then, national politics had always seemed to me a necessary and highly amusing but relatively unimportant aspect of the American way. Now it became vital; the country looked to its politicians for real leadership. Having, as result of the crash, nothing much left except debts and leisure, I spent most of my time with politicians talking about politics. My debts were so formidable that I couldn't do anything much about them, anyway, except worry. Why, I asked myself, worry about my own debts when I could just as well be big and unselfish and worry about the whole nation's debts? So I went in for national politics with Byron Patton Harrison, senior Senator from Mississippi, as my guide and almost constant companion.

I had known Pat Harrison somewhat back home in Mississippi, but not as I came to know him in Washington. There will never be another quite like him. He was both statesman and pixie, a man of sharp intelligence and tongue, gentle humor, and enormous courage and integrity. Pat could never quite bring himself to be completely serious about either his associates or himself, yet he could be almost morbidly concerned about the welfare of his county. He could be sentimental and cynical all in the same mood.

Once, when quite young, I heard him introduce the late William Jennings Bryan to an audience that filled the courthouse square in my home town. He knew that Bryan had to catch a train in about an hour. His introduction took most of the hour. A neighbor of ours told me later that he enjoyed Bryan's speech very much but asked "who was the old baldheaded fellow who talked after Bryan had made the main speech?"

In the years of jolting transition from high prosperity to depression—from Republican to Democratic rule— Pat Harrison was the gadfly hectoring the elephant. He baited the Republicans both on the Senate floor and at the Burning Tree Country Club, which had been organized by Republican statesmen for Republican statesmen. Harrison was one of the few Democratic members, and I became another. Having been a star baseball player in Southern leagues, Pat readily adapted his reflexes to golf. The money he took away from Senator James Couzens, Assistant Secretary of Treasury Ogden Mills, and other well-heeled Republicans at Burning Tree was something of a share-the-wealth project in itself. Pat was almost as good at the bridge table, and with the same results.

On the Senate floor, his speeches were the best shows Washington of that time had to offer. They packed the galleries and delighted the press. He would hold forth at length on Agriculture Department pamphlets as examples of the sort of thing the Republicans were spending the taxpayers' money for. His best speeches were on pamphlets called "The Love Life of the Bullfrog" and "How to Dress for a Sun Bath." There was sting and an undercurrent of seriousness in them, but they didn't leave scars.

How much they had to do with the downfall of the Republicans in the 1930 Congressional elections is problematical; they certainly didn't help the GOP, but it was already on the skids as a result of the depression and President Hoover's insistence on helping distressed business through the Reconstruction Finance Corporation while opposing direct assistance to the unemployed through the kinds of relief agencies Franklin D. Roosevelt was to set up later.

After one of his speeches, Harrison strolled across the Senate floor to the Republican side and whispered in the ear of Senator James Watson of Indiana:

"Jim, ain't I the worst demagogue you ever heard?"

"No, Pat," Watson replied, "I am."

This was the same Jim Watson who was described by Senator George Moses of New Hampshire as "that delightful old fraud." Watson at about this time was caught taking stock from a corporation he had presumably done some favors for. Explaining himself on the floor, Watson said he had done nothing for the corporation, that its stock had been worthless, and therefore that he had got nothing for doing nothing and everybody concerned was even.

When the hard-pressed Republicans got to fighting among themselves, it was Moses who insisted, after one of their stormiest caucuses, that they had been "wading knee-deep in harmony" and who characterized GOP mavericks of the La Follette-Norris-Brookhart school as "Sons of the Wild Jackass."

51

The Senate in those days was, in fact, what it has often been called since but never again has been—the World's Most Exclusive Club. Members were friendly and to a large extent in agreement on fundamentals. Many of them were rich men who had spent their own money getting elected. As result of the direct primary system, which was intended to make the Senate more democratic, the Senate had become an expensive association that only the rich, the clever, or the lucky could join and consequently, of course, somewhat less democratic than it had been before. Moreover, good times had made for a relaxed atmosphere in the upper branch of the legislature. All that seemed needed for several years was enough restraint in the lawmaking process to leave the country's enterprisers free to create and distribute wealth unlimited.

Another of my favorites of that time was the blind Senator from Oklahoma, Thomas P. Gore, a Democrat. Once I called on him in his office and, to make conversation, asked him whether he had any opposition that year.

"Yes, George," he said, "I have a fellow running against me."

"What sort of fellow?" I persisted.

"Well, I'll tell you," Gore mused. "I don't want to be hard on him, because anybody has a right to aspire to a place in the Senate, even my place. I would say of this fellow that he has every attribute of a dog except loyalty."

Then there was the time that Senator Furnifold McLendell Simmons of North Carolina, onetime undisputed boss of his state, sent a batch of communications to the desk for reading by the clerk. The communications endorsed in fulsome terms some bill Simmons was trying to put over. But after a few of these, the reading clerk intoned: "The Honorable Senator Furnifold McL. Simmons, Washington, D. C. My dear Senator: Your note of last year is now past due, and we would appreciate your advising us when you intend to pay. . . ." Simmons broke in at that point: "Mr. President," he shouted, "that's the wrong letter, and I want it expunged from the record."

Things went from worse to horrible for the country and for its Republican rulers in the months leading up to the Congressional elections of 1930. These elections threw the Republicans out of control of the Capitol, so Harrison became chairman of the Senate Finance Committee and John Garner, who was then considered a dangerous radical, became Speaker of the House. Franklin D. Roosevelt was re-elected Governor of New York that same year. Although he was still thought of as a rather weak, rich man, whose principal claim to glory was his "Happy Warrior" speech nominating Al Smith for the Presidency in 1928, some Democrats were beginning to be convinced that he would win the nomination in 1932 and win the Presidency over Herbert Hoover. Pat Harrison was one of those who thought so, and he threw his considerable political weight on that side of the scales. Because of Harrison, I was automatically for Roosevelt, too, but, since I was a citizen of the voteless District of Columbia, my political weight wasn't even one vote.

I regretted that, because I was getting pretty seriously

concerned about politics. I was a married man now, and the future looked bleak, not only for the country but for me. Harrison, who had been best man at my wedding, kept telling me that my golf and bridge were good enough to assure me a fair income as long as the Republicans stayed in Washington, but it was obvious that few of them would be staying after the next Presidential election. I needed something more substantial than a career in bridge and golf.

The Chicago Convention, that July, was a solemn depression affair. I went to Chicago with Harrison, Holly Stover, and Joe Davies, and we put up at the Congress Hotel. One of the first Chicago friends I ran into was Walter Gregory, who was then running the Palmer House. When I asked him whom he favored for the Democratic nomination he replied: "Deadlock." He said the convention, however it came out, would be a godsend to the Chicago hotel business if it lasted more than a week. It was a godsend to all of us, if for no other reason than that it got us out of Washington, which by then had the bonus army in its back yard and the Hoover Administration in its front yard. They were equally depressing. The Republicans couldn't do anything right. They tried to be optimistic too long. Hoover, himself, vetoed a relief bill; he seemed to lose no chance to identify himself with the depression. Hoover was, I have always felt, just as sincere as the Democrats in his determination to relieve distress and cure the depression, but his honest conviction that relief should trickle down from the top, not up from the bottom, made him seem callous and stubbornly wrong-headed.

Harrison had his hands full at Chicago because Mike Connor, at that time Governor of Mississippi, who favored Newton D. Baker over Roosevelt, kept trying to switch the delegation away from Pat's choice to his own. On the first night of balloting Harrison and I left the convention hall thinking there would be an adjournment, only to learn from the radio, after reaching our room, that there would be another roll call that night. Pat rushed back and found, as he had feared, that Mississippi was preparing to follow Connor into the Baker camp, but succeeded in holding it in the Roosevelt column. He realized, after that, that Roosevelt would have to be nominated the next day if he was to be nominated at all. Jim Farley, Louis Howe, and Frank C. Walker, Roosevelt's floor managers, arrived at the same conclusion.

Garner, who was the Hearst press' candidate, had the votes to swing it to Roosevelt. So it was arranged that Silliman Evans, the publisher, and Sam Rayburn, the Texas Congressman, would meet the leaders of the Roosevelt campaign in Harrison's and my room that night. This would be technically neutral territory and, more important, it wouldn't attract the attention of the press, as would a meeting of this kind in Garner or Roosevelt headquarters. Before the Garner representative arrived, Jim Farley asked Pat: "What shall we offer them?" Pat, sage old political war horse that he was, gave the only possible answer: "Anything they want."

The rest is history. The next day the Garner delegates swung to Roosevelt on the fourth ballot and gave him the nomination. As it turned out, the Garnerites didn't want anything. At least they didn't ask for anything as the price of their support. Roosevelt paid them by asking that Garner be nominated for the Vice-Presidency, but so far as I know he was not committed in advance to do so, although it was taken for granted that he would. Later the conservatives in both parties did a lot of worrying about Roosevelt's health, particularly after an attempt was made on his life in Florida, because they dreaded the succession of as radical a man as Garner to the Presidency. They still looked upon Roosevelt as a conservative and an economizer and something of a weakling. But these illusions didn't last long.

CHAPTER 6

I'll Be Good
to Them Dogs

THE year 1933 came in like a mangy, ill-tempered lion. Iowa farmers threatened to lynch insurance-company representatives trying to evict them; a clownish little man wearing a Charlie Chaplin mustache and a greasy raincoat dissolved the German Reichstag; America waited impatiently for March 4, the day Franklin D. Roosevelt would replace Herbert Hoover. When Inauguration Day came at last Roosevelt told the country in that soothing, reassuring voice of his that it had nothing to fear save fear itself. An impressive group of heavy thinkers moved into the capital in Roosevelt's train—Raymond Moley, George Peek, Hugh Johnson, Henry

57

Wallace, Rexford Guy Tugwell, Jerome Frank, Adolf Berle, and scores more.

A fellow from Chicago named Harold Ickes, who had been under consideration for Indian Commissioner, suddenly found himself Secretary of Interior, to his ever-lasting amazement and joy. Homer Cummings, an old friend whom I had first met when he was Chairman of the Democratic National Committee in 1920, came to Washington to be Commissioner of the Philippines, but remained to be Attorney General when Senator Thomas Walsh of Montana died on his way to the Inaugural. Young Theodore Roosevelt, who had been Hoover's representative in the Philippines, was asked at about this time whether he was related to Franklin D. "Yes," he said, "I'm fourth cousin about to be removed." Hoover had appointed Theodore Roosevelt in happier times, be-fore the characterization, "the great engineer," became a title of derision. In those better days, Hoover is sup-posed to have had some fun in him. Some people even give him credit for several good stories about Calvin Coolidge, his predecessor. One of these had to do with a proposal that a well-known captain of industry be placed in Coolidge's Cabinet. A Coolidge associate had objected: "But, Mr. President, that fellow's a son of a bitch." "Well," Coolidge replied, "don't you think they ought to be represented, too?"

Everybody who hadn't been anybody was going into the government service. I began to feel like one of the money-changers they were driving from the temple—a feeling made worse by the lack of any money to change. The hotel business still wasn't much; the inrushing Democrats needed housing but also needed the wherewithal for accommodations. One day, riding out to the Burning Tree Country Club, I said to Pat Harrison: "Pat, why don't you get me mentioned for District Commissioner? I don't want the job, but I could use the publicity."

I thought I was making the kind of jesting proposal that can be bandied about through a round of golf and then forgotten. Pat played up to it, and we speculated for a while on the kind of things I could do to enliven the Washington scene if I were one of the three District of Columbia Commissioners who run the nation's capital city. There must have been sixty applicants for the jobs, and the Washington newspapers were intensely interested in Roosevelt's possible choices. The day after our golf game Pat ran into Gould Lincoln, political writer for the *Washington Star,* and told him he was overlooking a hot dark horse—a fellow named George Allen. "Who's he?" asked Lincoln. Pat told him—with imaginative embellishments. Lincoln wrote the story, and other Washington papers followed his lead.

Whereupon an amazing thing happened to me. I was completely taken in by my own publicity. I convinced myself—and without an argument—that public duty was summoning me to the supreme sacrifice. I, George Edward Allen, was the fellow Uncle Sam was pointing at in those First World War posters captioned: "Uncle

Sam needs you." I read the names of distinguished Washingtonians mentioned for Commissionerships and said to myself: "How can Roosevelt consider those stuffed shirts when I am available? What a disaster the appointment of any of those men would be to the good people of Washington!" It didn't occur to me that I knew nothing about police or fire protection, traffic control, or even garbage collection. Pat reminded me of all this several times, but I was not even amused. He also warned me solemnly about the deadly political virus and what it could do to a man, particularly an Allen. My mind may have told me, "no, no," but there was "yes, yes" in my heart. Finally, after several months of waiting, Roosevelt awoke to his plain duty and appointed me, wholly on Pat's say-so and Jim Farley's seconding; the President didn't know me from George Spelvin. But he was to have that well-nigh unbearable pleasure later.

My sense of mission had developed quite a wingspread by the time I moved into the District Building. And it kept growing after I got there. For I was dumped headfirst into the sobering problem of unemployment relief. My office was besieged from the very start with the victims of America's worst depression. They were all kinds of people—veterans left over from the bonus army, the habitually unemployed, middle-class people to whom deprivation was not only an unaccustomed hardship but an outrage to dignity and respectability, former government employees who had served their country well, most of them in inconspicuous jobs but some of them in places of high responsibility, learned men, and professionals. It was a heartbreaking and frightening experience. What was to happen to a country that, though blessed with plenty, couldn't take decent care of its own? This was a situation about which I managed no feeling of jocularity then and cannot now. I sometimes see in my mind's eye those rows of hopeless men and women when the Monday-morning quarterbacks tell me how many mistakes Roosevelt made in the early days of the New Deal— when they tell me that all our present troubles stem from Roosevelt's softheadedness in launching the welfare state at the bottom of the depression.

Careerists in the lower echelons of the government have a bad enough time even when they're employed and secure in their jobs. I remember once, years ago, dining at the home of Merle Thorpe in Bethesda, Maryland, with a visitor from England. When darkness came, the Britisher was fascinated by the twinkling display put on by the lightning bugs and asked whether it would be possible to transplant some of them to his place in Surrey. Since nobody at the party was familiar with the requirements of the lightning bug, we referred the Englishman to the Agriculture Department. There, the next day, after a long hunt through endless corridors, he found the office of the department's lightning-bug expert, who gave him a two-hour discourse on the ways of the flashy insect. At the end of the lecture, the visitor thanked his instructor profusely for the enlightenment.

"But you must not thank me," the expert protested.

"Permit me to thank you. I've been here for thirty-five years studying lightning bugs, and this is the first time anybody has ever asked me anything about them."

I hadn't been in office fifteen minutes before Harry Hopkins, a newcomer to Washington then himself, appointed me Relief Administrator for the District of Columbia. It soon developed that I wouldn't have much time to learn about police and fire departments, street sweeping, and garbage disposal. My colleague, Melvin C. Hazen, the other Commissioner appointed when I was, had been in the public service for years and was a master handler of these normal city problems. (In fact, he had first gone to work for the District government a few years before I was born.) He managed that part of the job without any help or interference from me. I became the guinea pig on whom Hopkins tried out relief schemes later applied to the rest of the country if they worked, and charged off to experience if they didn't. Hopkins became a close friend during this period and remained so through the next fifteen years, until his death. I soon learned that one of his weaknesses was his golf game, which was not only bad but extraordinarily bad. To Harry, any shot was successful if the clubhead hit the ball. I once spotted him two strokes a hole with the understanding that he'd give me an additional million dollars for District relief projects if I won, as I did on the eleventh hole and as he, of course, expected me to.

No President ever had a better kitchen cabinet than I had as District Commissioner. It was composed of the newspapermen who covered the District beat, the equivalent of the city hall in any other town, and their unemployed colleagues whom I put to work as reliefers on various writing and research projects. They were given the run of my office, and my desk drawers and records were always open to them. Robert Buck, a newspaperman out of the Charlie MacArthur-Ben Hecht school of *Front Page* journalism, had been a Chicago councilman and was the nearest thing to a genius I've ever known in matters of municipal politics. He was also the strangest combination of hard-boiled cynicism outside and sentimental kindliness inside. He became my unofficial prime minister, and I never got a bad piece of advice from him.

Bob Buck was always after me for something, but never, I observed, for himself. He not only favored the underdog, but seemed to know a kennelful of the species personally. When the job of District pound keeper opened up, Bob knew about it, naturally, before I did and had a candidate for the office ready and waiting when I found out about it. The applicant was a deserving citizen named Marks. When I asked him about his qualifications, he said, "Commissioner, I don't know much about it, but I'll sure be good to them dogs." He was and still is.

I had a lot of trouble with one of the first Civil Works Administration projects I launched—a playground-improvement program. The city playground department didn't think much of it, but my relief department thought it had done a splendid job. So I laid on a tour of inspection to settle the argument. It was done in my usual self-effacing way—with reporters and photographers from the four newspapers, press-association representatives, and radio commentators all there by urgent invitation. I looked things over and decided that the playground department was finding fault out of bureaucratic stubbornness with a perfectly good job. But when I told Bob I thought so and meant to say so, he whispered: "Say it's a lousy job but you'll try to do better next time." "But it's a good job," I insisted. "Say it's a lousy job and you'll try to do better next time," he repeated. Against my own judgment, I took the prime minister's advice and as a result got a terrific press. Here at last was a public official who could take criticism in good part and learn from it, the newspapers agreed. How refreshing! What a splendid public official! Bob came into my office the next day with a Mona Lisa expression on his face and asked me the secret of my success. I explained to him that it all stemmed from my innate modesty. He walked out to see if he couldn't spot an opening for one of his unemployed acquaintances.

I had several of his friends working at the time on so-called white-collar projects. They were doing histories of the District of Columbia, making library surveys to find out what people read and what not. It was difficult to think up enough tasks for brain workers because, like manual workers, they didn't like idleness, popular opinion to the contrary notwithstanding. Finally, I thought up a dandy project. I set some of the newspapermen

with decent sporting instincts the task of finding out
how many favorites had won over the last twenty years
of turf history at the more reputable tracks. They found
that thirty-three per cent of the favorites won, but not
with any consistency, pattern, rhyme, or reason. The
study confirmed a cliché: you can't beat the horses. I
was satisfied with the moral, which I have never taken
to heart, even though I had hoped the boys would dis-
cover some foolproof formula for cashing tickets. I had
told them that what I wanted was a system that would
make us all lots of money, part of which we would pay
to the government in taxes and thus create a pump-
priming pool. I make no apology for what will seem to
some a horrible example of boondoggling. The problem
was to save human beings from feeling useless and hopeless. If research in horse racing could do this, then research in horse racing was justified. I am forced to concede, however, that this was one of the schemes Hopkins
didn't adopt for the rest of the country.

I was interested enough in the problem of unemployment relief by this time to have a close look at the way
other cities were handling it, so I set out by bus for Cleveland, Toledo, Detroit, Chicago, and Milwaukee, posing
as an unemployed waiter.

At the Statler in Cleveland I applied to the bell captain
for a job as bellboy. He asked where I had worked before,
and I told him at the Stevens in Chicago. He asked me if
I knew Bill Cunningham there. I assured him that I
knew good old Bill intimately. He said I was a liar be-

cause to his certain knowledge there wasn't any Bill Cunningham in the employ of the Stevens. Job lost. In Detroit I tried to pawn my watch, for which a friend had paid $150, but kept it in my pocket when the pawnbroker said he couldn't give me more than four dollars on it. In Milwaukee, forgetting my shabby appearance, I walked in the front door of the Schroeder Hotel. I got a sick feeling from the peremptory order of the doorman: "Hey, you. The back door."

After being kicked out of a number of the hotels I had patronized at various times, insulted by social workers, and turned down by twenty-five employers, I returned to Washington to recommend some drastic changes in administrative methods to Harry Hopkins. My principal recommendation was that he order his people not to act like God Almighty. And, incidentally, I told my experiences to the Washington press. I have a clipping of the *Washington Star*'s two-column front-page spread on my own account of my adventure. The last line quotes me thus: " 'Please,' Allen added, 'don't make me out as doing anything melodramatic.' " That must have been a Bob Buck suggestion. All accounts were extremely—and gratifyingly—melodramatic. Except Pat Harrison's comment: "George, I knew you were a bum, but I didn't know you'd advertise it."

As a result of this experience, I had a modest part in helping to plan the work-relief program President Roosevelt adopted in 1935. It was a program to give real work instead of doles to all employable unemployed. Its original cost was $4,800,000,000, and I have always thought it was worth it. At the press conference at which he announced it, the President told reporters that it had come out of a recommendation from me. But when the reporters came to me, I had not been advised in advance that the White House had approved release of my memorandum to the President. So I pretended to have forgotten it. The *Washington Post* commented editorially at the time:

"If Commissioner Allen ever writes his memoirs, he may well record his interview of Wednesday as one of life's darkest moments. For the Commissioner was then suddenly catapulted into national distinction by a brain child which, apparently, he did not recognize. . . . He appears to have been somewhat bewildered when he discovered that his casual ideas about work relief were to become the guiding light in the President's plan to spend $4,800,000,000."

By this time, my public relations were so good that they started making me all sorts of troubles. When a carpenters' strike shut down all construction in Washington, including work on the executive wing of the White House, a job close to Roosevelt's comfort, the *Washington Herald* published an editorial suggesting that I offer my good offices as conciliator, since I enjoyed the confidence of both labor and contractors. Forgetting the advice of an old friend down home who said he had made a fortune minding his own business, I charged into the labor dispute and got negotiations so tangled that within a few days all the building trades were on strike. Finally, Bill Hutcheson of the Carpenters' Union straightened things out, but not until I had cost his dues-paying members a lot of man-hours. Later, Senator James Couzens of Michigan told a mutual friend that I was the man to settle the sit-down strikes—that I could get the men out of the factories, and keep them out, if anybody could.

Pat Harrison, meanwhile, was having his troubles with Theodore Bilbo, who was in Washington at a loose end, having served out his term as Governor of Mississippi. Cole Blease and Tom Heflin were passing from the scene by this time, so Bilbo was one of the last of the Claghorns. He was a little man who looked insignificant, but he was a master of the Southern brand of demagoguery and a shrewd political manipulator in any arena. Because he would have given Harrison a hard battle for re-election, Pat was eager to keep Bilbo in Washington. He did this for a time by giving Bilbo coffee-and-cake handouts. But this became irritating, not so much because of the out-of-pocket cost as because of the necessity of seeing and talking with him at frequent intervals. So Pat talked George Peek into giving Bilbo a job in the Agriculture Department.

Pat explained to Peek that Bilbo was a splendid Democrat, a party man of enormous achievement, an expert on the agriculture of the South, and a deserving fellow all around. It would not be a good idea, Pat said, for Bilbo to be permitted to run around making speeches, particularly in Mississippi, to be given control over government money, or to be left alone with pretty stenographers.

With these statesmanlike reservations, however, Bilbo was eminently fitted for any position the Agriculture Department might have. Peek listened to the sales talk and then said: "In other words, Senator, this good Democrat, Bilbo, will be fine for us if we muzzle him, tie his hands, and lock up the petty cash." Harrison conceded that he had the right idea, and Peek gave Bilbo a job clipping, and pasting in scrapbooks, items from newspapers bearing on the Agriculture Department's various activities. Bilbo called himself the Pastemaster General and drew his pay until the time came to run for Senator against Hubert Stephens, then Harrison's Senatorial colleague from Mississippi. Pat supported Stephens, but Bilbo won and then tried in every way possible to eliminate Harrison by running Governor Connor against him.

At Pat's invitation, I went to Mississippi with him at one point to do what I could to help in his campaign and at the same time to see how the farm program was going in the South. While in Baldwin, I ran into an old farmer friend and asked him why he hadn't gone to Tupelo to attend a big farm meeting the Agriculture Adjustment Administration was putting on that day. "I don't want to go," he said. "But," I objected, "here's the government spending a lot of money to teach you farmers better agricultural methods, and you don't even go. Why not?"

"Shucks," he explained, "I ain't farming as good as I know how now."

Pat was re-elected without any trouble. The Harrison-Bilbo feud had interesting repercussions later when Democratic Leader Joseph Robinson of the Senate died in the midst of Roosevelt's court fight. Harrison, because of seniority and capacity, was the logical successor to Robinson, but the President thought him too conservative to fight the Administration's battles in the Senate, so he endorsed Alben Barkley of Kentucky for the job. In the scramble for votes, which started among the mourners on the Robinson funeral train, Senator James Byrnes of South Carolina, who served as Harrison's campaign manager, lined up enough support to assure Harrison's election by one vote—or thought he did. But Harry Hopkins went to work on Edward Kelly, the Democratic boss in Illinois, and swung William H. Dieterich, one of the Illinois Senators, to Barkley. An attempt was made at the same time to reach Senator Harry Truman through Tom Pendergast, the Missouri boss, but Truman had given his word to vote for Harrison and refused to consider a switch.

After discovering that Dieterich had changed sides, Byrnes went to Bilbo and asked him if he would consider voting for Harrison. If he would, Harrison could still win the majority leadership, a job he very much wanted. Bilbo said he'd support Harrison if Pat would speak to him. (The Mississippi Senators hadn't been on speaking terms since the Harrison-Connor primary.) Pat said he'd think it over. He wrestled with himself in the privacy of his Senate office for about a half-hour and then called Byrnes and said: "Tell the son of a bitch I wouldn't speak to him if it meant the Presidency of the United States."

So Barkley was elected by one vote, and, of course, made a distinguished record. In view of the closeness of the vote and of his warm personal regard for Harrison, Barkley said he felt like a man who was being ridden out of a Kentucky town on a rail and replied to a bystander who asked him how he liked it: "If it wasn't for the honor of the thing, I'd just as soon walk."

My own job as District Commissioner was going fairly well, but it was getting me lots of other incidental work. Whenever President Roosevelt had some semiofficial chore to do—and he had many of them—he got in the habit of turning it over to me, probably because I was handily underfoot. Thus I became involved with the Red Cross, the March of Dimes campaign, an international Boy Scout jamboree, and scores of similar enterprises. My friends got to teasing me about neglecting my important duties for all these relatively unimportant sidelines. They gave me a small private dinner one snowy winter night at Gus Buchholtz's Occidental Restaurant. It was supposed to be a testimonial dinner, but turned out to be a testament to my shortcomings. One of the guests was Will Rogers, who, in the closing speech, said the real purpose of the affair was to find out whether Commissioner Allen could get to the dinner through the drifted snow left on the streets by his own negligence.

Through the whole depression period everything was secondary to the business of supplying jobs. Private industry simply couldn't do it; the government had to. Private employers were forced to slash their payrolls. John J. Pelley, president of the Central Railroad of Georgia, who had been laying off help with the rest, told a story on himself that illustrated the primary problem of the times.

Going to his office early one morning, Pelley heard two Pullman porters talking. One of them told the other he'd had a frightening dream the night before. He had dreamed that President Pelley was dead and that he had gone to the funeral. As the casket was being borne to the grave, Pelley's corpse lifted the lid and asked how many pallbearers there were. When told that there were six, the corpse ordered: "Let two go."

The 1936 Presidential election proved, if any proof were needed, that Roosevelt's policy of attacking unemployment and depression with aggressive Federal measures was what the country wanted. It was too bad that so nice a fellow as Alf Landon of Kansas had to be the victim of this demonstration of the voters' liking for Roosevelt. I remember Dorothy Thompson telling me at a 1936 dinner party that if Landon made another speech Roosevelt would carry Canada, too.

The story is told that Landon and Mrs. Landon swore

they'd leave Kansas if he failed to carry this, his own home state, in the election. When the returns were all in, and he had carried only Maine and Vermont, Landon called home to find out whether his wife remembered their pre-election vow.

"Yes, I do and I'm all packed," she said.

"You better unpack, dear," Landon suggested. "There's no place to go except Maine and Vermont, and they're too cold."

CHAPTER 7

I Kick Myself
to Sleep

PEOPLE have all sorts of curious ways of judging other people. Some contend that the eyes are windows to the soul. Others hold that the contour of the chin reveals everything. Housewives used to judge each other by the condition of their rivals' soap dishes. I have no confidence in any of these methods or a hundred others I have heard of. I judge a man (or a woman, though that is more difficult) by the sort of thing he laughs at. When a funny bone is most sensitive to whimsy, to the scatological jest, to the shaggy-dog story, or to the comedian's ludicrous hat, or to any other subdivision of humor, I catalogue the owner of the bone accordingly. The kind of joke a man laughs at and the way he laughs at it tell me almost all I need to know about him. It tells me whether, by my own unexacting standards, he is kind or cruel, intelligent or stupid, complicated or simple; it also suggests gradations. I shall not go into details of my method here. Perhaps I can sum up my system best by stating simply that I like most the people who laugh hard at my jokes and that I like least the people who don't laugh at all.

What I am getting at is that by these standards Franklin D. Roosevelt was a man I instinctively didn't rate high. I had to learn to like him as one learns to like olives. I had to keep telling myself in his presence that this was a great man, a man who was saving America from itself, a man of good will, a man of the highest character and most subtle intelligence. I discovered upon closer acquaintance that he was capable of infinite kindness as well as greatness. But the fact remained that he laughed only perfunctorily at my jokes, and I tried all varieties on him. Even worse, he responded with bad jokes of his own, and then I had to laugh at them more convincingly than he had laughed at mine. Roosevelt could be a delightful conversationalist and companion, as I found out gradually over the years I served as District Commissioner, but he was most charming when he was most serious and least so when his mood turned playful, as it sometimes but not very often did—fortunately, I think.

To be brutally blunt about it, he was a practical joker. What the practical joker enjoys is the discomfort of his victim. Several times I was the butt of Roosevelt's practical jokes and, while I didn't suffer intensely, I didn't enjoy myself either. Perhaps my victimization had something to do with my lack of appreciation of the jokes.

After completing a political survey of the West during one of the Roosevelt campaigns, he persisted in being more optimistic than my reports gave him any right to be. So I told him the well-seasoned story, then making the rounds, about the Congressional candidate who called at the Jones farm while all the menfolk were in the fields. Mrs. Jones reviled him, set the dogs on him, and shouted at his fleeing form that she wouldn't vote for him if he were the last man on earth. Returning to his car, he took out his canvassing list and marked after the name of Mrs. Jones, "doubtful." That didn't even get a polite laugh, but maybe Roosevelt had heard it before.

He was also cold to another of my favorites—the story of the colored slave who had achieved something of a reputation as a weather forecaster. His method was to consult the ache in his bones. Finally, a publisher who offered to put the old man's predictions into an almanac was directed to include the forecast: "Atlanta, for mid-August, sleet and snow."

"But how can you predict sleet and snow for Atlanta in August?" the publisher objected. "Nothing like that has ever happened."

"Well, boss, it probably won't happen this time either," the predictor conceded. "But if it do I'll be the damnedest prophet that ever lived."

I had been Washington chairman of the President's Birthday Balls from their beginning in 1934, working

closely with Basil O'Connor, Roosevelt's former law partner and later head of the American Red Cross, and Mrs.
Roosevelt. They were more elaborate affairs in the capital
after 1935, when I arranged with Woody Van Dyke, one
of the top directors at Metro-Goldwyn-Mayer, to send
movie stars to Washington to provide glamour for a city
where other kinds of public personages were a dime a
dozen and therefore not glamorous. That first time we
got Jean Harlow and Robert Taylor. When I called Mrs.
Roosevelt to suggest that she invite these two attractive
young people to tea, she declined but suggested instead
that she have them to lunch and invite the press, too.
That luncheon became an annual affair, as did Mrs.
Roosevelt's evening rounds of the hotels where the balls
were held. I customarily accompanied her on these rounds
and always enjoyed them up to the point where I became completely exhausted fighting crowds and pumping
hands. It was at about this point that Mrs. Roosevelt was
getting well started. Once I stopped her short by standing
on the train of her gown, but I had to step off before I
could get any real rest out of the slowdown. Out of the
idea for the Birthday Balls came the National Foundation
for Infantile Paralysis, now one of the largest of the char-
itable foundations and one I still serve as a director with
deep satisfaction.

In his book *Dear Mr. President,* Ira R. T. Smith, who
had been chief of the White House mail room for many
years, told what havoc the first appeal for dimes wrought.
According to Smith, I had told him: "You may get a

trickle of dimes in the mail." Knowing very little about the power of radio, a trickle was, in fact, all I had expected. Instead, it turned out to be a tremendous flood that all but inundated the executive offices.

As a result of suggestions by Eddie Cantor and the Lone Ranger that their listeners send dimes to President Roosevelt, White House mail increased from a normal 5000 letters a day to 30,000 the first day after the broadcasts, 50,000 the second day, and 150,000 the third day. Before it was over, 2,680,000 dimes came in. As Smith puts it: "We kept on getting incredible numbers, and the government darned near stopped functioning because we couldn't clear away enough dimes to find the official White House mail."

Everybody available around the White House was pressed into service as a mail sorter. Even Sam Rosenman, the President's speech writer in chief, and Mrs. James Roosevelt went to work in the mail room. In subsequent years the White House made special arrangements to handle the March of Dimes mail, which by 1950 was producing more than $30,000,000 a year for treatment of polio victims and for research.

Smith writes: "I never saw George Allen after that without a shudder. A 'trickle of dimes' indeed!"

With Keith Morgan, an important contributor to the success of the National Foundation for Infantile Paralysis in its early days, I was making a tour to inspect orthopedic hospitals for the Foundation in 1937, and we found ourselves in Denver when the President's special train came through Colorado en route to the West Coast, where Roosevelt had arranged a vacation cruise. Roosevelt invited us to join him for the ride to San Francisco, and we boarded his train at Cripple Creek, Colorado, the day Supreme Court Justice Benjamin Cardozo died. The newspapermen aboard the train, most of them old friends of mine, accused me of coming to get Cardozo's job, and immediately started a mock campaign to persuade the President to appoint me to the vacancy. I was appointed chairman of the campaign finance committee and ordered to put on a champagne dinner to get things started. Everyone got in the game of thinking up arguments and qualifications, including the President.

The first night, after the train had stopped on an out-of-the-way siding and the President was presumed to be asleep, Steve Early, his press secretary and one of my oldest and best friends, announced over the train's loudspeaker system, in tones and accents that imitated the President's perfectly, that he took pleasure in announcing the appointment of George E. Allen to the United States Supreme Court. The press crowd in the dining car applauded. The trouble was that the President, awaking, heard the announcement, too. But he said nothing about it until the train reached Sparks, Nevada, the next day. He then asked me to join him on the rear platform while he made a little speech to the 10,000 people gathered there to see him. My mind wandered as I heard him delivering the usual informal rear-platform talk but was brought back with a jolt by the words: "And now, ladies and gentlemen, I want to introduce a good friend of mine, Judge George E. Allen, of the District of Columbia, who will now say a few words."

The newspapermen led a stirring round of applause, and I was thrust forward. With some difficulty, I managed to get across the thought that I was glad to be there. The President looked solemn, and a visiting Nevada politician offered congratulations. While the train was pulling out, and while still shaking slightly, I recalled an old jingle:

> *Oft in the stilly night,*
>   *Ere slumber's chain has bound me,*
> *I think of things I should have said*
>   *When others were around me.*
> *And of such woeful waste of wit*
>   *Constructively I weep,*
> *And often in the still of night*
>   *I kick myself to sleep.*

While I was doing this, Roosevelt laughed harder than I ever heard him before or after. From then on Roosevelt called me Judge Allen, and his secretary Grace Tully still does.

Years later, shortly after Pearl Harbor, I encountered Norman Davis, head of the Red Cross, one day at the Burning Tree Country Club. He took me aside and asked how I'd like to go to Ireland on an important mission for his organization. The ostensible purpose of the trip was to find out what Red Cross supplies Ireland would need and whether its sweepstakes-financed hospitals would be thrown open to Allied wounded, but the real purpose was to give Irish-American relations a little shot of blarney at a time when Eire's neutrality was threatening to become troublesome. I was wined and dined by Prime Minister de Valera and members of his cabinet and toured the country with Chief Justice Connor Maguire of the Irish Supreme Court.

Maguire had a bottomless fund of stories about his own experiences as a revolutionary. One of his favorites concerned a dissatisfied client. Maguire had defended this man against charges growing out of revolutionary crimes. In spite of the lawyer's best efforts, the man had drawn a long prison sentence. When, later, Maguire himself was sent to the same prison because of anti-British activities, the client shouted at him from a cell block: "You must have been your own lawyer."

Another Maguire story had to do with the conversation of a group of Free Staters assigned to assassinate a pro-British landlord. The assassins designed an ambush at a street corner their victim habitually passed every night, but on this particular night he failed to show up. "I hope," said one of the cutthroats solicitously, "that nothing has happened to the poor old fellow."

I was certain before I left that Ireland would come into the war on our side, merely on my say-so, and was somewhat surprised to observe, as the war dragged on, that Ireland's neutrality held firm. Anyway, the flight to Ireland

and back over an ocean that was an active part of the battleground seemed quite hazardous to one who at that time dreaded an air trip from Washington to New York. So I returned to Washington brimming over with information about the Irish situation and with a sense of virtuous achievement.

I didn't quite know how to make my report or to whom. I consulted my friends about it and rehearsed privately. My first opportunity, it soon developed, was to be at a welcome-home dinner at Burning Tree arranged by Steve Early and Sam Rosenman. Many Administration bigwigs were to be present to hear what I had to say about the Irish situation. I naturally looked for my place card at the speaker's table when the guests assembled, but failed to find it. Finally, I was ushered to a small table segregated from the other diners. I was forced to listen to a long program of speeches about the failure of the Allen Mission to Dublin and then, when at last called upon, I was left standing while the guests, by prearrangement, walked out muttering to themselves. It was an elaborate rib.

Some days later I was in Canada with Harold V. Smith, president of the Home Insurance Company, my boss and personal friend, when the White House telephoned that I was to return at once to report to President Roosevelt on my Irish mission. I, of course, hastened back to Washington. Presenting myself at the appointed time the next day, I was told that I would have a half-hour and to cover as much ground as I could in that time. I was ushered in by Pa Watson, Appointment Secretary. The President, after greeting me and complimenting me on my services in Eire, started talking about trivialities in an animated way. This went on and on. Every time I opened my mouth to say something about Ireland, the President was reminded of something else he wanted to say. At the end of the half-hour, Watson came in and announced that my time was up. Then Early and Rosenman burst in to join in the laugh and to advise me to put my report in writing.

I then told them an Irish story to illustrate my opinion of them. It concerned an Irishman named Tim McGuire, the principal speaker at an affair intended to conciliate the forces of Ulster. McGuire began his conciliatory speech with the preamble: "I have never said an unfriendly word against Orangemen—misguided, bigoted, and besotted though they be."

But my White House visit did give me a chance to make my recommendations concerning Eire to somebody of importance. While I was waiting in an anteroom for my appointment, Lord Halifax, the British Ambassador, was ushered in to do the same thing. As usual, President Roosevelt was behind his schedule of appointments. Cornered and helpless, Lord Halifax listened while I told him rather more about the Irish question than he wanted to know. I have always chosen to assume that His Majesty's Government profited from Halifax's report on my expert recommendations, although I have never seen any evidence that it did.

In 1938, after serving five years as District Commissioner, I decided to return to private business as a vice-president of the Home Insurance Company. I had done what I could for the District, but I was forced to confess to myself that it hadn't been much. There wasn't a great deal anyone could do for a city that was run by Congressmen and Senators who were elected by the citizens of other communities and who regarded their responsibilities as councilmen for the District either as a nuisance or as an opportunity to prove something or other for the benefit of their own constituents. What they usually proved was that they were willing to make drastic budgetary economies if it didn't hurt their own chances for re-election, and in the District it didn't.

I wanted then and still want District citizens enfranchised. At the 1936 Democratic Convention in Philadelphia, I put on a Boston Tea Party with some Indians whose co-operation I had enlisted for that purpose. We made lots of noise and got a hearing before the platform committee and a resolution in the platform. After one of our no-taxation-without-representation demonstrations in the lobby of the Bellevue-Stratford Hotel, a kind old lady congratulated me. She said she agreed with me that the Indians should be allowed to vote. We had made a point, all right, but not the point we wanted to make. Citizens of the District still can't vote.

Harry Butcher, then a vice-president of the Columbia Broadcasting Company, took charge of arrangements for an elaborate farewell dinner to mark the end of my public service. With two-dollar contributions solicited from my friends, he purchased a desk set for presentation to me at the dinner. Its plaque was inscribed: "To the Honorable George E. Allen, presented by those who knew him best (consequently, the binding is done in brass), in appreciation of his Resignation as Commissioner of the District of Columbia." Harry Hopkins, Jesse Jones, Jim Farley, Steve Early, Joe Tumulty, Joe Davies, Pat Harrison, Pa Watson, Jim Moffett, Jim Roosevelt, Merle Thorpe, John Pelley, Marvin McIntyre, Grace Tully, Missy LeHand, and many others in and out of the Administration were among the donors.

Senator Fred Hale of Maine wired that he wouldn't be able to attend the dinner, "relieved as I am to get rid of George." He said he'd try to attend, however, when the insurance company got the same break the people of the District were getting. The only solemn note was struck by Joe Davies in a message from Belgium, where he was then serving as Ambassador, warning in language only slightly veiled that a European war was just around the corner. Along with the desk set, I was presented with a bill for the dinner.

After I had been out of office a year, President Roosevelt negotiated with the Home Insurance Company for a "short-term loan" of my services to reorganize the District government. About a year later, after I had submitted my report, I retired permanently, even though the Washington papers suggested that I probably would do as many farewell tours of duty as Sarah Bernhardt. Our reorgani-

zation bill, as presented to Congress, was analyzed by
Homer Cummings. In a private letter to me, he said, in
part:

DEAR GEORGE:

The longer I know you the more I find my affection
for you mingled with awe as I contemplate your
unique and varied achievements.

Recently I have been giving further study to Senate
Bill #3425, two copies of which I enclose herewith. It
seeks, so its caption proclaims, "To provide for the
reorganization of the government of the District of
Columbia."

And what a reorganization! It is a reorganization to
end all reorganizations!

The more the Bill is studied the more its inward
unwholesomeness is revealed.

Almost every Section carries an open or covert attack
on our most sacred liberties.

The only sensible provision in the entire Act is to be
found in Title II, Section 201, page 3, line 19, which
states "The term 'District' means the District of Columbia."

This is clear, explicit, and understandable.

Out of abundant though unnecessary caution, the
provision of the Bill just quoted is repeated in Section
701, page 34, line 15, viz., "The term 'District' means
District of Columbia."

Moreover, in Section 802, page 38, there is further

indication of malign purpose. This Section provides as follows:

> The powers and authorities conferred by this Title are to be construed as in addition to and not by way of limitation of the powers now vested by law in the Commissioners.

The motive is manifest. The Commissioners, meaning, of course, George E. Allen, have not only all the powers heretofore granted "by law" but all other powers in addition thereto of every kind and description. The movement toward autocracy is unmistakable.

However, the culminating and most grievous insult to the body politic, to all right-thinking people, to all who love liberty and revere the founding fathers, and especially to those political expendables and social untouchables, without vote, power, or influence, who reside and pay abundant taxes in the District of Columbia is contained in Section 802, Subsection (*u*) on page 44.

I pause to weep before I proceed further.

This provision authorizes and empowers the Commissioners "within their discretion" (mark the potent words, "within their discretion") to issue permits, and I quote literally,

> for the removal from place to place, inter, disinter, or in any manner dispose of any dead body or *any human being or any part of such body,* and to prohibit the removal of any dead body *or any human*

being or any part of such body without a permit granted under such rules and regulations as may be prescribed by the Commissioners.

No living person, to wit: "any human being," can no longer go and come as he chooses. He must ask your permission to move about, to go to any Government Building, Rock Creek Park, or the washroom. No one can die without your consent. No deceased person may be budged, transported, or manhandled without your assent.

Pause, my friend, ere it is too late, or we shall cry, with Cassius, "Upon what meat does this our Caesar feed that he is grown so great?"

Speaking as an elder statesman to a neophyte, I warn you against the dangers of excessive legislative adulation. No doubt you revel in it, but it is a toxic agency which works corruption in the blood. I tremble for the safety of the Republic of our fathers.

Sincerely but regretfully yours,

HOMER CUMMINGS

On that note my career as District Commissioner ended.

CHAPTER 8

Optimism Has Me
by the Throat

I LIKE to think of myself as a hardheaded American businessman—aggressive, enterprising, and sound. But I also like to feel that I have the additional something that makes the difference between an ordinary, hardheaded businessman, like many others I know, and an extraordinary, hardheaded businessman, like me. That additional something, I tell myself (usually while shaving), is imagination. Sometimes I go further and call it a sense of adventure. It is the thing that makes me willing, even eager, to take risks. It gives me something the pioneer had. It makes an enterpriser of me. It is the quality that made America what it is today. It is the thing that has led me to invest in gold mines, oil-drilling enterprises, inventions of various kinds, including a perpetual-motion machine, and, on occasion, in the animals called horses which run around oval roads called race tracks. Put another way, it is what has made me a prize sucker.

I do not, of course, like to think of myself as a prize sucker. But I've come to the conclusion that you can fool some of the people all of the time, and that I'm one of them. There are occasions (most often upon returning dispirited from a hard day at the races) when I am forced to look the bitter fact in the face. At these times I tell myself that I am a softheaded American businessman—gullible, romantic, and unsound. Why, I then ask myself severely, did I ever harbor the stupid notion that a thirty-to-one shot could win the last race and pay me back all I had dropped on favorites that somehow failed to pay off in the earlier races? Ordinarily I am ingenious enough to blame my bad judgment on a tout, but not always. Fortunately, however, my capacity for self-reproach is not robust. It never survives a good night's sleep. By morning, optimism again has me by the throat.

After all, the difference between a bold enterpriser and a sucker is no more than the thickness of a cigarette paper. The American who looked at an unappetizing grain of rice and had the imagination to see that he could make a fortune by blowing air into it and advertising the resulting globule as a muscle-building breakfast food was pretty much the same kind of fellow as the American who had the vision to look upon a field horse and imagine himself collecting sixty dollars on a two-dollar ticket. Yet the rice popper was an enterpriser who became a respected millionaire, and the long-shot horse player is a ne'er-do-well who becomes a bum. The difference between them is only that the bet on blown-up rice paid off whereas a bet on a long shot doesn't, at least not often.

So I shall not apologize for being a lifelong devotee of long shots. I'd be better off today if I had just bet on them; my biggest indiscretion, and my costliest, was trying to own a few of them. I didn't do too badly when I merely yielded to greed by betting on horses in the hope of getting rich quickly and without effort. It was when I yielded to the temptation to become a respectable horse owner and so contribute to the improvement of the breed that I plumbed the depths. It is impossible to hate a horse until one has raised one—and raced him. He can be poetry in fast motion when he belongs to somebody else, but he can be an oats-destroying monster to his owner.

Let it be said in my own defense that I got into racehorse owning by accident rather than design and in extenuation of my folly that I displayed real cunning getting out of it. Mel Hazen, a Virginia gentleman and, naturally, a horse breeder, was responsible for my original lapse. It had been a dull meeting of the District of Columbia Commissioners, and Commissioner Hazen, by way of making small talk, suggested that Commissioner Allen owed it to himself, being a horse player, to be a horse owner. By happy chance, Hazen had at the time a horse named Worthowning which he would sacrifice for a mere eight hundred dollars. More to keep the conversation going than anything else, an old trouble of mine, I said I'd buy the horse if Hazen would come down to a more reasonable six hundred dollars. First thing I knew we had split the difference and I had become the owner of Worthowning for seven hundred dollars. That very afternoon Worthowning won a three-hundred-dollar purse at Marlboro, a half-mile track in Maryland called the poor man's Santa Anita. That evening I congratulated myself on my acumen as a horse trader, and I was in for it.

It is one of my misfortunes that I always have friends ready to encourage any delusion I happen to be harboring momentarily. This time the friend was Johnny Gheen, who had another friend who had some splendid race horses he was willing to sell at a great personal loss. The reason for Johnny's friend's willingness practically to give these horses to me, as I remember it, was that he was having trouble with his third wife. Somebody has said that a third marriage represents the triumph of hope over experience, and the race horses probably represented a similar victory.

In any case, I soon found that my horses were costly to keep, so I bought a farm for them. I was like a man who, having acquired a yachting cap, had to buy a yacht to go with it. When the war came along, I was wise enough in the ways of government to foresee that horse racing would be banned for the duration, so I decided to quit racing my horses before it became necessary and devoted my farm to the more serious business of raising the food that would win the war. Accordingly, I had my broad acres planted to corn. For the first time in seventeen years, the Potomac flooded its banks, carrying my corn seed down to the Atlantic for fish feed. The following year, betting that the river wouldn't flood two years in succession, I doubled the corn planting, to make up for the previous season's loss. That was the drought year, and my corn seed was eaten by the crows.

Meanwhile, my farm manager, who had overlooked the fact that race horses were similar to birds and bees and other creatures in their procreative processes, turned the girl horses out with the boy horses. The result was a big crop of hungry foals that would have to wait until the end of the war to carry the Allen silks. Incidentally, the government, in its wisdom, decided not to discontinue horse racing during the war, on the theory that it was important as a home-front morale builder.

Soon after I acquired my first race horse, but before I had bought him companions and a farm, the question of building a race track in the District of Columbia was brought before Congress. As a Commissioner, I testified against the proposition. I told members of the Senate District Committee at a formal hearing that Washington was inhabited principally by modestly paid government employees who shouldn't be encouraged to lose their paychecks on horse racing, as they would be if the sport were brought to their own doorsteps. At this point Senator Robert Reynolds of North Carolina demanded to know whether I was not myself a race-horse owner, and I had to admit that I was. I tried to cover my embarrassment by assuring Reynolds that I owned only one horse and that I would gladly give it to him if he'd accept it. To my amazement, he said he'd always wanted to own a race horse and, in fact, a race horse was just what he needed.

A few days later Reynolds went with me to the old Bennings race track in the District of Columbia, where Worthowning was stabled, to meet my horse personally. In the stall with the horse when we arrived was a malodorous goat—a mascot and horse companion thrown in with Worthowning in the original Hazen deal. Reynolds looked over the two animals and said he'd prefer the goat. Since the Washington press was out in force to witness our transaction, I had to give him the goat. I hated to do it because I was myself quite fond of the goat, on which I had never lost any money. The headlines on the sports pages were so obvious that I am reluctant to quote them, "Senator Gets Commissioner's Goat."

My successes as a player follow very closely my triumphs as an owner. Once at Belmont, I was touted on a long shot that couldn't possibly lose unless he broke his leg. The tout was so convincing that I plunged on the horse. He led all the way and literally broke his leg just short of the finish line. Even so, his momentum was such that he placed. I had bet him to win. Then, one winter, Steve Early and I went to Florida and lost so steadily that we had to cash a check at our hotel every morning before going to the track. When we checked out, flat broke, the hotel clerk had the bad taste to ask: "Do you gentlemen have anything hot running today?"

I once knew a druggist who lost everything he had following the tips of a particularly persuasive tout but still couldn't stay away from the races. He liked to go just to watch the horses run. One day when he was just watching, the tout who had cost him so much suggested that he place a mental bet on a sure thing. This was too much. The broken druggist shouted, "You make me lose my money, then my drugstore, and now you want me to lose my mind."

The farm I bought my race horses in Montgomery County, Maryland, its thousand acres of green field rolling down to the Potomac, was one of the most beautiful I ever have seen. I was considerate enough to take Harold V. Smith and Wilfred Kurth, two business associates, and Frank C. Walker, the then Postmaster General, into partnership with me in this farming venture. We tried everything, from Henry Wallace's hybrid seeds to the latest in electrical milking machines. We hired a manager who was so scientific that none of us could understand what he was talking about. Mrs. Allen said she was always a little embarrassed to note that the landlord couldn't follow the multisyllabic talk of his farmer. Even the government compensation checks didn't do much for us. Finally, we gave my assistant, Ed Reynolds, a Harvard man who until then had known farms only as the things you see from train windows while traveling through the Middle West, the job of running the farm. He abandoned science, followed the common-sense practices of our neighbors, and put our enterprise in the black—barely. Feeling that we had licked the problem, we then sold out before the locusts—the only blight that had not yet descended—noticed their oversight.

I have never appreciated landscapes, however glittering, since that experience. But I am still holding onto stock in a Montana gold mine that has never paid a dividend owing to circumstances over which the management has no control. I also am in on an oil-wildcatting syndicate that recently drilled a hole on a piece of ground literally surrounded by producing wells. Another friend of mine let me in on this deal. I wouldn't take anything for the fascinating progress reports I still receive. These reports telling why there is no oil where oil simply has to be can take their place, unashamed, in the world's best literature of frustration.

It should be a matter of gratification to all Americans, particularly taxpayers, that I exercised my talent for finding good things in the public interest while in government service. On one occasion I found a French explosives expert who had a fiery liquid with which he promised that the United States Air Forces could easily burn out all enemies, particularly the Japanese, whose wooden houses would be tinder. He all but started a forest fire demonstrating his stuff to our chemical warriors along the Potomac. I never knew why our people seemed unimpressed until I found out that at the time of this demonstration they were working on the atom bomb, a more impressive weapon.

And after the war, as an RFC official, I brought out of

Germany two scientists who said they had discovered a way of obtaining energy from the air—a discovery that would revolutionize industry and transport. I didn't get suspicious of these geniuses until Max, the temperamental one, insisted upon going from Ohio, where he had been installed in a laboratory, to California, where the climate would be more conducive to proper functioning of his great brain. Eventually, our scientists discovered that my Germans were selling an idea based on the pipe dream of perpetual motion. We sent them back to Bavaria. Today they may be in Moscow, telling the Russians how to extract energy from the air. I hope so.

I shall not labor further the point I am trying to make—that as a businessman I am not the conventional banker type that demands six per cent interest on his money and adequate security; that I am a venture capitalist of the more uninhibited variety; that it is men of my forward-looking and overreaching stripe who have been responsible for building America. I sometimes think that ours is a dying strain, and I often think how fortunate that is. The country has all the race tracks and crispy, crunchy breakfast food it needs.

PART THREE

CHAPTER 9

The Fellow to Watch Is a Brigadier General Named Eisenhower

THINKING back, I find it difficult to remember whether I actually had a prescient feeling that war was coming or whether I only thought I had felt it coming after it came. All I can be sure of is that I wasn't completely bowled over by the news of Pearl Harbor that Sunday afternoon of December 7, 1941. I knew that Saburo Kurusu, the special envoy from Japan, was in Washington and that the negotiations weren't going well. Moreover, some years earlier I had known Japanese Ambassador Hirosi Saito and I had never forgotten his private predictions that something like Pearl Harbor would happen if the military continued to guide the destinies of his country. He had been stanchly pro-American and anti-Japanese militarist, at least in his talk.

Steve Early and Marvin McIntyre, President Roosevelt's secretaries, and I took on Saito for a foursome at Burning Tree one afternoon and refreshed ourselves with a few drinks after playing eighteen hot holes. Perhaps we overrefreshed ourselves. In any case, we happily accepted Saito's gay invitation to go home to dinner with him. His wife, he told us, would be enchanted. At Mac's insistence that it was the right thing to do, we took off our shoes before entering the Embassy. Saito sent a servant to get his wife.

She looked at her husband and his three shoeless friends and, like an American wife in similar circumstances, was not enchanted. She reminded the Ambassador that he could change in time, if he hurried, for the formal dinner party he had forgotten. Later Madam Saito and Mrs. Allen shook their heads sadly over the affair, and we all became good friends.

Saito talked with me often about the intricacies of Japanese imperial politics. He was fearful, he said, that the military bosses of Japan would one day kill him. He was even more fearful of war between the United States and Japan. I never quite knew how literally he meant what he said.

He died suddenly in Washington, presumably of natural causes, some time before Pearl Harbor. Madam Saito told Mrs. Allen that the new Ambassador, who represented the military, had directed her to return to Japan at once with her two small daughters. She was afraid to go, but had decided to follow her husband's body, then aboard the U. S. battleship that President Roosevelt had ordered to transport the dead envoy to Tokyo. Madam Saito was sailing on another ship, which was to follow the battleship. Thoroughly alarmed, Mrs. Allen called me at my office and issued a peremptory order: "Stop the battleship." I tried to explain that I wasn't the Secretary of Navy, but in the end I did tell Madam Saito's story to a friend in Secretary of the Navy Charles Edison's office, and the battleship conveniently developed engine trouble while the high brass decided that it had no choice but to send the Saitos home. The mission ran about a month behind schedule.

In the days leading up to Pearl Harbor I had troubles of my own, but Pearl Harbor was big enough to overshadow them. No lesser disaster would have. My troubles derived from a small incident. Mrs. Allen and I were spending a few days in New York with Mr. and Mrs. Harry C. Butcher. Butch was conferring with broadcasting people, and we were helping him compound business and pleasure. One evening as the four of us walked through the revolving door of the Ambassador Hotel on the Park Avenue side, a blowzy blonde, whose appearance left no doubt about her profession, sang out a "Hello, George." Butch thought it was a great joke and spent the rest of the evening asking me who my friend was. Mrs. Allen didn't think it was a great joke and spent the rest of the evening asking me nothing. Shortly things arrived at the point where nobody believed the assurances of the doorman that his name was "George" and that the woman had been addressing him. Although the evidence was purely circumstantial and would have no standing in a court of law or equity, I had to concede that I wouldn't have believed me, either. Mrs. Allen, assisted by Mrs. Butcher, picked up her handbag and went home to Washington. Butch also returned.

Left alone, I sought solace at Ben Marden's Riviera, just across the George Washington Bridge in New Jersey, where there was then illegal gambling. I was sitting at a roulette table when somebody remarked that President Roosevelt had sent a message to the Emperor of Japan over the heads of the military. "We shall be at war in twenty-four hours," I said, probably to relieve my own gloom by borrowing trouble for others. The next day Pearl Harbor was attacked. Mrs. Allen called me from Washington to say that, angry as she still was, she'd be willing to declare an armistice in our war until after the country's war was won.

After listening to long months of wrangling between isolationists and interventionists at home and to news of new triumphs for Hitler abroad, it was almost a relief to be at war—to know where we stood and what we had to do. Having been wholly in sympathy with Roosevelt's effort to assist the Allies by every means short of war and willing to go to war, if necessary, to prevent the Nazis with their racial fanaticism and the Japanese with their

strong-arm imperialism from grinding the Americas between two deadly millstones, I was eager, as almost all
Americans were, to get into the push. That was why I
seized upon the Irish assignment mentioned previously.
While all I was supposed to do was court Irish good will
and arrange to supply hospitals with necessary medicines
and equipment from the United States, I nurtured the
hope that my mission might produce some further dividend for the Allied cause.

In my determination to be properly prepared I col-
lected letters of introduction to Irish personages from
their friends in the United States. Postmaster General
Frank Walker, whom I consulted about this project, suggested that I call upon Archbishop Spellman and ask him
for a letter of introduction to the Archbishop of Dublin.
When I did so, Spellman asked me about Joe Cronin, an
outstanding Washington ball player who had been sold to
the Boston Red Sox. I then recalled that I had dined at
the White House one night in 1936 with Mrs. Allen,
Missy LeHand, General and Mrs. Watson, Jimmy and
Betsy Roosevelt, and a bishop from Boston with whom I
had discussed Cronin. It had been Bishop Spellman, now
Francis Cardinal Spellman, and he had remembered not
only me but our conversation. I was impressed. I remembered the story John S. Burke, who runs B. Altman's in
New York and was then head of Catholic Charities, told
me about Cardinal Spellman. One night his telephone
rang, and Mrs. Burke answered. The voice emanating
from the receiver said: "This is Cardinal Spellman." Mrs.

Burke gasped: "I can't believe it." The Cardinal said: "Neither can I at times."

After I returned from Ireland, Cardinal Spellman graciously sent me a letter he had received from Archbishop John C. McQuaid of Dublin, thanking him for my visit. Archbishop McQuaid reported that "it would be difficult for you in the United States to realize the sympathy his visit has evoked." I have often wondered what His Eminence meant.

Because of the kindness of the Archbishop, of Foreign Minister de Valera, and, indeed, of all the people I met while making a tour of inspection of hospitals, I was persuaded that Eire could be brought into the war, thus shortening our Atlantic supply line, giving us additional staging areas and ports and not inconsiderable help in fighting manpower. It occurred to me that this might be achieved by indirection, if the direct approach failed, by encouraging Pan American or some other private company to build a new airfield in Ireland and, in effect, inviting the Luftwaffe to attack it. I was convinced that the Irish would repulse any such attack and that, in so doing, they would force themselves into the war.

During my month in Ireland this idea grew upon me. So, without consulting anyone in our government, I decided to take it to London before returning home. I still have the top-secret document outlining my views to Brigadier General Robert A. McClure, who officially transmitted them to the chiefs of our military mission in London, discussed them in Washington with Harry

Hopkins, and later outlined them to General Dwight D. Eisenhower. This document proposes construction of commercial airline landing strips in Ireland, supply of certain arms to the Irish Army, establishment of Allied convalescent centers in Irish hospitals, and use of Irish ports. I felt not only that Ireland might be useful to the Allies, but that its continued neutrality might be dangerous to Britain—that it might be a convenient stepping-stone for German invasion of England itself.

While in Ireland, I told everyone I talked with I didn't mind having the Irish neutral so long as they were neutral on our side. And, so far as I could see, they were. I didn't talk with one Irishman who wasn't sympathetic with the Allied cause.

But my plan to lure the Irish into the war struck an unexpected snag very quickly. Ambassador John Winant informed me that the British wouldn't be willing to permit us to arrange for construction of commercial airports in Ireland because they already were thinking about their own postwar commercial air prospects. That was a time when it seemed touch and go whether there would be an England after the war to worry about commercial airlines or anything else. I was profoundly shocked. But I have since concluded that the British were wise to think about some of these postwar prospects during the war. Some of our own postwar troubles might have been less severe had we done the same thing. It is now perfectly plain, for example, that our failure to prepare for the Soviet Union's imperialistic drive for territory after the armistice should have been foreseen by our leaders and prepared for. Winston Churchill alone, among the wartime leaders, seems to have had the foresight to anticipate Russia's behavior after the war, but even he didn't consult his own forebodings seriously enough.

General James E. Chaney, who was then in command of U. S. troops in England, Ambassador Winant, David Gray, our Minister to Ireland, who visited London while I was there, Tony Biddle, then our Ambassador to European governments in exile, and his wife, Margaret, were all intensely interested in developments back home and wanted to talk about the United States as much as I wanted to talk about Ireland. At dinner one night Winant and Biddle asked me who the upcoming men in the army were. Who would be the European Commander? They couldn't have consulted an informant with less information. I had few acquaintances and fewer friends in the armed services. I hadn't the foggiest idea. But they wanted gossip from home, and I tried to accommodate. I remembered reading shortly before I left the United States that an officer named Eisenhower had won some war games in Louisiana as commander of the Red or the Blue forces; I couldn't remember which. "The fellow to watch," I told them, "is a Brigadier General named Eisenhower. He's a great soldier."

The next day Winant called me, highly excited. "Why didn't you tell us General Eisenhower was coming over here to take command?" he asked. For a half minute I didn't know what he was talking about. I'd forgotten mentioning the name. "You, of course, knew it last night when you were talking about him," Winant chided. "Don't be so cagey."

"Well, I can't tell you fellows everything I know all at once," I answered.

From then on, in the American colony in London, I was the man who knew Eisenhower, who had recommended him, and who was responsible for his appointment. The more I assured my friends that I didn't know the General well, the more convinced they became that I was his advance agent on the scene. The fact was that I had met Eisenhower, if at all, only in the most casual way, although Mrs. Eisenhower and Mrs. Allen were friends. I didn't even remember what he looked like. I began to see that it was going to be embarrassing for me when the General showed up in London not even knowing who George Allen was. But I breathed easier when I got a message from home telling me that my old friend Harry Butcher had been appointed Eisenhower's aide.

So when Eisenhower and Butcher arrived, I stated my problem. I told the General he and I were supposed to be old friends and I was perfectly willing to be his old friend if he'd co-operate to the extent of playing up a little to the innocent deception. He seemed to be amused by my plight and said he'd gladly take me off the hook. In fact, he'd put on a demonstration of our comradeship by taking me to lunch at Claridge's, where our association would be witnessed by a maximum number of important and efficient gossips. So I enjoyed a delightful luncheon with Eisenhower, General Mark Clark, and General T. J. Davis on perhaps the only occasion when Eisenhower dined publicly in London.

After that, I spent much time with the General and Butch. Indeed, I became Eisenhower's most enthusiastic self-appointed unofficial adviser on the conduct of the war. I was pessimistic. I told him Hitler was going to take the Suez and bottle up the Mediterranean, invade Ireland and cut off the United Kingdom, knock Russia out of the war, and proceed to mopping-up operation in all directions.

All my gloom seemed to make the General more buoyant. His perverse attitude reminded me of a story about my uncle John. Once in Washington, after the Civil War, he was approached by a panhandler—a Union war veteran who had fought many battles and showed the marks of every one. Uncle John gave him five dollars, which, at the time, was a lot of money. Overcome more by curiosity than gratitude, the veteran asked why his benefactor had been so generous.

"Because," said Uncle John, "you are the first Yankee I've ever seen who was shot up to my complete satisfaction."

Butch recounted some of our conversations in his war diary, later published as *My Three Years with Eisenhower*, and noted: "If a war could be made happy, George could do it. He was a good tonic for Ike." As a matter of fact, I wasn't feeling happy about the war at the time and I probably needed tonic worse than the General did.

And I got it. He was and still remains one of the most confidence-inspiring men it has been my good fortune to know. If he ever entertained the slightest doubt about the outcome of the war, he never betrayed it by so much as a crease in the forehead. He never underestimated the difficulties, but neither did he question the ability of the United States and its Allies to meet and overcome them. I was so impressed with his determination that I told him about Knute Rockne's contempt for the "good loser." Rockne wanted nothing but "bad losers." Good losers get into the habit of losing. Rockne wanted boys who would tear their hair out by the handfuls on the rare occasions when Notre Dame lost.

All this was in June, 1942, and Eisenhower had agreed to speak at a Red Cross meeting on July 4. Determined that Ike should do well with this address, one of his first abroad, Butch and I went to work doing a ghosting job. We spent long hours on the address and, when we were through, confidently adjudged it a masterpiece. The General was properly grateful. With such a writing team, he said, he'd soon establish a reputation as an orator. Butch and I began to think of ourselves as another Sherwood-Rosenman combination. He made a speech all right, and it was a masterpiece. But there wasn't a word of the Butcher-Allen script in it. It was a ten-minute off-the-cuff talk about the Allied cause. It was an inspiration to England particularly and to the whole free world. It was simple, from the heart, and eloquent. I recognized then a fact that my experience with General Eisenhower has since confirmed: that he needs a ghost writer about as much as I need more starch in my diet.

I wrote no more speeches for the General and gave him no more military advice, but on May 23, 1943, I received a tongue-in-cheek letter from him paying tribute to my services as a military adviser. I once entertained the idea of putting this letter away in a safe-deposit box with instructions to the bank to open and publish it one hundred years hence, with the object of baffling historians. The letter said:

DEAR GEORGE:

In your letter of May 4th you said: "We are expecting great news any day now."

I hope you are satisfied with the news you received.

I am sure you recognize in this campaign the grand strategy and tactics which you so carefully and so enthusiastically advocated while you were in London. Your advice was of incalculable value to the Allies!

If you have any other suggestions, I would appreciate having them, preferably in person.

Sincerely,

IKE

Eisenhower was referring, of course, to the successful conclusion of the North African campaign. He was then getting ready to push on into Italy before returning to England to plan the Normandy landing.

I was fortunate enough to draw another Red Cross

assignment, this one having to do with care and exchange of war prisoners, in the summer of 1944, just before the Normandy kickoff. As a result, I was with Eisenhower and Butcher at the General's temporary headquarters in the south of England at invasion time. By then buzz-bomb raids were making London and its environs remarkably uncomfortable, and I had what I considered at the time some close calls. As I remember it, I was forever trying to get under something on that visit to London, even if the something was only a seat in a flimsy British taxicab.

I made myself as useful as I could at Eisenhower's camp near Plymouth. When Butch and the General were out I kept a watch on their telephones and when they were in I tried to take their minds, at least for a few moments, off the tremendous task in which they were engaged. Knowing the General to be a bridge fan, I got up a game as often as possible. A few nights after D-Day, I persuaded him and Butch and James Galt, Eisenhower's British aide, to join me in a game in the General's trailer. On the first deal, I drew the joker and protested that we were using the wrong kind of deck. "Wrong deck, nothing," said the General. "This is our only deck. The joker is the six of clubs, which is missing."

Those days, the General divided his time between Telegraph Cottage, which was just outside of London, and his temporary headquarters near Plymouth. One day the two of us were having lunch at Telegraph Cottage when the alarm sounded for a buzz bomb. We sauntered toward a bomb shelter. That is, General Ike sauntered, and I couldn't very well besmirch the Allen military record by running ahead of him. So I sauntered too, desperately. But when the second warning sounded, an orderly suggested that the General run for it. My feet, overhearing the orderly before I did, carried me to the shelter well ahead of the General. I accidentally shut the shelter door in his face, locking him outside. The bomb, fortunately, fell some distance away.

Realizing what I had done, I gave serious consideration to spending the rest of the war in that dugout. But I had to brazen it out. So I walked out with dignity, looked the General in the eye, and said to him severely: "Sir, you'd better practice your starts."

Few men, I should think, have ever been burdened with a heavier load of responsibility and anxiety than General Eisenhower during those days immediately after the invasion. Any one of a hundred mishaps could have made the grand undertaking a disaster rather than the tremendous victory it was. Some of the hazards lay beyond the control of Eisenhower or any other man. The weather, for example. Eisenhower had made the decision to invade in the face of unfavorable weather reports. The night a storm in the English Channel partially destroyed the artificial harbors floated across on D-Day, Eisenhower slept not at all. But his determination to carry off the invasion, quite literally in spite of hell and high water, never wavered.

Watching him through all this, I kept trying to remind myself that I was seeing history in the making. But what

I kept thinking was: man at work. Here truly was a man, a great man, at a great work.

General Eisenhower's wartime role, in spite of all that has been written about it, has been widely misunderstood. Much has been made of his achievement in holding the anti-Axis alliance together at the top strategic level. Much also has been made of his contribution as a morale builder. Actually, these services of his, while important, were incidental to his main job. He was a soldier; he had spent his life preparing for the responsibility the war thrust upon him. He was a military commander and a military strategist. He was one of the architects of the grand design for Allied victory. Not only did he help write the over-all blueprint, but many of the war's most important decisions were made by him in the field.

The Combined Chiefs of Staff, who were the top planning body, and his only military superior, learned to trust him completely. They never made a decision affecting his area of command without consulting him. Probably no other commander of modern times has been accorded so great a degree of independence in decision and execution as he was.

One of Britain's top military men once said this to me in trying to sum up Eisenhower's value to the Allied cause: "Our great need, we all soon discovered, was a man—and a genius was sent to us by God."

What impressed me was the greatness of Eisenhower as a person. Things never got so thick that his thoughtfulness of others failed him. And his thoughtfulness was more than just good manners. It was deep within him, a compulsive thoughtfulness. I left him twice at times when he was busy and harassed. On one occasion he got up hours before his usual rising time to see me off; the other time he personally took me to the station. In the midst of war's preoccupations, he had time to be the perfect host.

This may not be very important in itself, but it is an indication of the kind of man Eisenhower is. He comes as close to being selfless as anyone I have ever known. In the war, he served only one master: the Allied cause. In peace, he is serving only what he conceives to be the good of his country. He refused the Presidential nomination in 1948 for one reason and only one. There need be no mystery about it. He refused because he didn't think it would be wise of the American people to pick as President a man they knew only as a military leader. He wouldn't let them make their selection on that basis. If such conduct is too unworldly to be credited by politicians, then they will never understand Eisenhower.

I have seen a lot of him since the war. We have talked American politics endlessly, played bridge and golf together, hunted and fished together. He is good at everything he does; indeed, he insists upon being good. He swears off golf at least once every game because he isn't as good as he thinks he should be, but, of course, doesn't quit. Recently much of his diversion has come from painting, which he took up after the war at the suggestion of Tommy Stevens, an artist he likes, who has painted his portrait several times. Even as a painter, he is beginning to acquire considerable skill.

Had Eisenhower been persuaded to submit to a Republican draft in 1948—and it would have had to be a real draft—I should still have voted for President Truman. Eisenhower knew this, and, of course, it has not interfered with our friendship in any way. He realizes that my affiliation with the Democratic party is as much a part of me as my bulging waistline.

But even my black Mississippi Democratic soul won't permit me to deny that the Republican party, had it got Eisenhower, would have had a candidate worthy of its Abraham Lincoln tradition.

CHAPTER 10

The Conspiracy
of the
Pure in Heart

IT is not like me to brood over yesterday's narrow escapes. I am ordinarily too busy dodging today's taxicabs to give thought to the hacks that almost ran me down yesterday. But there is one narrow escape that bathed the palms of my hands in cold sweat at the time it happened and still frightens me when I think of it. I sometimes awake with a start late in the night, when vitality is low and past fears parade themselves across the darkened bedroom wall, to find myself thinking of a day in 1944 when Henry A. Wallace came within a few votes of winning the Democratic Vice-Presidential nomination.

The Convention, partly out of admiration and partly out of pity, wanted to give it to him. He wanted it. Harry Truman, who had been thrust into the running against him, didn't want it. But for a little handful of men, who didn't want him worse than the majority did want him, Henry A. Wallace would have been nominated. Shortly thereafter he would have become President of the United States. What then would have happened to the United States is, of course, anybody's guess. I don't know, and neither does anybody else. My own ideas on the subject are what give me the chills when my own personal devils go marching by single file in that airless hour before dawn.

Until I can awaken enough to banish the vision and reassure myself that it didn't happen, I see President Henry A. Wallace sitting in front of a microphone in the Oval Room of the White House, reading a message to the peoples of the world. His forelock droops appealingly over his right eye. His flat Iowa voice proclaims that the United States of America shall henceforth be called the Soviet States of America, that all Democrats from Mississippi weighing more than two hundred pounds shall be rendered in order that unwashed comrades in Greater Russia can be assured an adequate soap supply, and that scientific socialism shall bring to the Western Hemisphere the same conditions that prevail throughout the glorious territories of mother Russia. It is all a silly dream, of course, but there it is. I am thankful for the occasions when I sleep right through until daylight.

Perhaps, as some of my friends contend, Wallace would have risen to the responsibilities of the Presidency, with all their sobering effects, had they been thrust upon him. I like to think so because there was a time when I considered him a highly appealing and useful public servant. But against this contention stands the evidence of the Wallace campaign of 1948, which was so openly run by the Communists and their fellow travelers that the fact of Wallace's captivity became obvious even to those who were most reluctant to see it—and finally, after the campaign, it almost seemed, even to Wallace himself.

Many accounts have been written of events leading up to the decision of the Democratic Convention of 1944 to shelve Vice-President Wallace and nominate Senator Harry Truman in his place. Some of them were written at the time by Washington correspondents who are normally careful, accurate, and understanding. Some have appeared since in the memoirs of men who were intimately acquainted with a part of the maneuvers— but not with all of them. I think I have read everything written on the subject, because it fascinates me. It is one of the episodes in American history that will baffle scholars of the future because no two accounts of it agree completely and some vary widely. I am not particularly worried about tomorrow's historians. It is not my ambition to make things easy for them. Let them work for their pay. Anyway, they'll pick the accounts that best suit their own preconceptions of what happened, as historians always have, and then defend their own pet versions in learned and heated tracts, thus holding their franchises as creative writers.

For strictly personal reasons, I am interested in the straight story of how Henry A. Wallace didn't become President of the United States. I like to tell it to myself periodically to convince myself anew that democracy, with all its faults, is a system that works; that democracy's politicians can be as strong and pure as Knights of the Round Table; and that a benign Providence, for all its absent-mindedness about the muddled doings of us mortals, does see us through the tight places.

By dint of great effort and much talk with the principals, I have now pieced together to my own complete satisfaction the straight story of Truman's substitution for Wallace in 1944. The heroes of my story are Edwin Pauley, the California oil man, who was treasurer of the Democratic National Committee when the noble deed was done; Robert Hannegan, who was then chairman of the Committee; Frank Walker, who was Postmaster General; Edward Flynn, Democratic boss of the Bronx, and Pa Watson. These men—all practical politicians and not generally regarded as idealists—entered into a sort of informal and idealistic compact to beat Wallace. All of them realized that the man nominated to run with Roosevelt would in all probability be the next President of the United States, because all of them saw enough of Roosevelt to recognize that his health had deteriorated rapidly

121

in the war years. They were determined that Roosevelt's successor would not be the boomerang-throwing mystic from the place where the tall corn grows.

It is my notion that a commemorative plaque honoring these five politicos should be erected in Potomac Park in Washington, but, of course, it never will be. The United States Senate, in its wisdom, refused to confirm Ed Pauley for Under Secretary of the Navy or Ed Flynn for Minister to Australia. It didn't consider them suitable for these high offices. General Watson died in the line of duty while returning from the Yalta Conference. Walker was preparing to resign his Cabinet post and take over Watson's less exalted position as Secretary to the President, the better to serve Roosevelt, when the President died. Hannegan worked himself to death in the service of the Democratic party. But they were mere politicians—mere practical politicians—and no sculptor will ever be commissioned by a grateful government to chisel heroic statues of them to join Wallace's likeness in marble in the Capitol's statuary hall.

The Sir Galahad of the righteous band that set out to beat Wallace was Ed Pauley. He was the knight with the shiniest armor and the sharpest spear. The trouble with Pauley was that he didn't—and still doesn't—cloak his aspirations and projects in fancy enough words. He talks about the anti-Wallace movement as a conspiracy and his associates in it as fellow conspirators. Moreover, he admits that he's a millionaire and that he made a lot of money by speculative plunging into commodity markets immediately after the war and refuses to see that there's anything questionable about making money and gambling with it as long as it's his own. He was the original anti-Wallace man in the Democratic-party camp. He picked up recruits as he went along.

For more than a year before the 1944 Convention he toured the country raising money for the party and, incidentally, mobilizing opposition to Wallace's nomination. As he went from city to city on party business he primed local leaders to mention to Roosevelt, when the opportunities presented themselves, that the Democratic ticket would suffer seriously from the presence of Wallace on it in the 1944 campaign. They were to tell Roosevelt that they were all for him but just couldn't stomach Wallace. Then Pauley made a deal with General Watson, a jovial soul who was called "Pa" by everyone around the White House, including the President, to clear the way for anti-Wallace Democrats to see Roosevelt when in Washington and to block the way for pro-Wallace Democrats on one pretext or another. Meanwhile, Pauley himself made the most of every opportunity to report on the extent and virulence of the anti-Wallace sentiment at the grass roots. Other Roosevelt men—including me, I must report in all honesty—were afraid to preach the anti-Wallace gospel to him because he had picked Wallace in 1940 and was sensitive about any criticism of his protégé. But that didn't stop Pauley. His arguments were forthright and telling.

It was not until he had to defend himself later before

the Senate committee considering his nomination for the second highest civilian job in the Navy that Pauley became inarticulate and seemingly defenseless. He couldn't cope with the testimony of Harold Ickes, who told the committee that Pauley had proposed to him in the summer of 1944 that California oil men be solicited for campaign contributions with a promise that the Federal government would abandon all claim to the underwater oil reserves they were tapping with the consent of the state of California, which then had control of these reserves. Two facts stood out in the resulting controversy. The first was that California oil men were not heavy contributors to the 1944 campaign. The second was that one of the first things Truman did after assuming the Presidency was to instruct the Justice Department to establish claim to the tidelands, which it did successfully in the courts. The case against Pauley always was implausible in the light of these facts. Pauley was nothing if not practical, and a practical man would scarcely have proposed this kind of deal if he didn't have it buttoned up to the extent of having the contributions lined up and an understanding with the White House and the Justice Department, as well as the Interior Department, not to press the tidelands case. Events showed that Pauley had neither the contributions nor the understanding. Yet Republican Senators chose to believe Ickes, in spite of these facts, and to disbelieve Pauley. As a result, Pauley was kept out of the Navy Department. This was probably unfortunate for the country. As strong a man as Pauley, backing up Secretary of the Navy James Forrestal, might conceivably have prevented Forrestal's tragic death and averted, or at least kept within reasonable bounds, the interservice row that so weakened the nation's defense establishment later on.

The political advisability of dropping Wallace and picking up Truman in his place was discussed at the White House as early as January, 1944. Pauley's one-man campaign already was bearing fruit. The President had talked with other party leaders about the problem of finding a Vice-Presidential nominee who would do the ticket more good than Wallace, who, although appealing to the CIO and left-wing liberals, would alienate middle-of-the-road independent voters, who had always supplied the margin of Roosevelt victories. Pauley, Hannegan, Walker, and Flynn were among the group that gathered with Roosevelt at an informal caucus in January. Some of them swear to this day that I was there, too. At that time I was secretary of the Democratic National Committee and often present at these meetings, but I am positive, after consulting my memory and my appointment slips, which are somewhat more accurate, that I was not.

The participants agree in a general way about what happened, if not about who was there. The Vice-Presidency and what to do about it was brought up. Several alternatives to Wallace, including Sherman Minton of Indiana, now Supreme Court Justice, James Byrnes of South Carolina, later Secretary of State, Justice William

O. Douglas of the Supreme Court, Speaker Sam Rayburn of the House, Senator Alben Barkley of Kentucky, and Senator Harry Truman of Missouri, were talked about. It was the consensus of the conferees that Truman would be the best bet, all things considered. He was making a respected name for himself as chairman of a committee policing war contracts; he was a loyal New Dealer but not a radical; he was from a midcontinental state. The President himself was favorably impressed with Truman's qualifications and said so. He also indicated that he agreed with the leaders that Wallace should be dropped in the interests of Democratic-party harmony. But no final decision came out of this meeting. Pauley, joined by Hannegan, campaigned openly for Truman after that but didn't claim Roosevelt's support and, indeed, didn't know for sure whether he had it.

That was the situation when I got back from England in July, only a few days before the Democratic Convention. Wallace was then on a tour of Russia and the Orient—out of sight but not out of mind. Harold Young, his political handler, was out working for Wallace delegates and doing fairly well at it in the absence of any authoritative word from the White House that Wallace was to be jettisoned. The official White House position was that the Convention would be left free to make its own choice of a man for second place on the ticket—a thing that is theoretically possible but that, as a matter of practical fact, never happens. The Presidential nominee always picks his running mate, one way or another.

Actually, domestic political maneuvers didn't seem all-important to me that summer. I left my primary interest in southern England, where I had seen Eisenhower sending our armies across the Channel for the Normandy invasion, and I read every scrap of news about their progress. But, of course, I accepted an invitation to a White House dinner for a few party functionaries on the night of July 11. President Roosevelt sat, as usual, at the head of the table. Ranged around it were Hannegan, Walker, Flynn, Kelly, Pauley, and I. John Boettiger, the President's son-in-law, joined us later. At dinner we talked principally about the war and listened to Roosevelt's reminiscences.

After dinner, over coffee and drinks in the study on the second floor, the talk turned to arrangements for the Convention in Chicago and, ultimately, to the Vice-Presidency. Again the field was canvassed. Brynes was ruled out because his nomination might be resented both by Northern Negroes, who had become an important factor in many industrial areas, and by Catholics, who would remember that he had been raised in a Catholic household but was now Protestant. Barkley was dismissed when Roosevelt remarked that the Kentuckian was older than he. Douglas appealed to the President because of his dynamic personality and his youth, which he had more of than anyone else. Roosevelt pointed out that Douglas had a kind of Boy Scout quality about him that might be appealing to voters and, besides, played an interesting game of poker. But the others were not enthusiastic. They said Douglas had no visible followers, with the possible exception of Ickes, who also had no visible followers, with the possible exception of Ickes.

That left Truman. The President recalled that he had approved Truman's selection for chairmanship of the Senate committee investigating war contracts and added that he never had regretted it. Truman was not only able and loyal to the Administration, he said, but was also wise to the ways of politics. But one thing bothered him—Truman's age. Whereas Douglas was under fifty, it was Roosevelt's impression that Truman was almost sixty. Knowing that this impression was correct, Pauley and Hannegan tried to change the subject, but Roosevelt suggested to Boettiger that he get a Congressional Directory and look up Truman's exact age. When Boettiger returned, Pauley grabbed the Congressional Directory and held it unobtrusively in his lap. Finally Roosevelt said to Hannegan:

"Bob, I think you and everyone else here want Truman."

At that point, still holding the Congressional Directory, Pauley hurried everybody out of the room before Roosevelt had a chance to change his mind. Downstairs, while we were getting our coats on, Frank Walker, probably one of the closest and most trusted friends Roosevelt had, suggested to Hannegan that he go back and get Roosevelt's implied approval of Truman in writing. Although Walker would have gone through fire for the

President, his loyalty didn't blind him to Roosevelt's propensity for changing his mind. Hannegan did go back on the pretext of getting his coat, which he thought he had left behind but which Ed Pauley had picked up by mistake while juggling the Congressional Directory, and got a one-line note penciled on the back of an envelope. It said: "Bob, I think Truman is the right man. FDR."

Roosevelt was now on record with the party leaders for Truman, but he still wasn't committed formally or publicly. The note was too personal and offhand to be of much real use. Roosevelt still was free to change his mind, and all those present at the White House meeting knew it. They also sensed that Roosevelt would not live much longer. At this meeting he had seemed tired and listless. Riding home that night, Frank Walker told me that he had never before seen the President stand on the sidelines and let others carry the ball as he had that night. I think all of us felt more strongly than ever that the man nominated for the Vice-Presidency would soon succeed to the Presidency if Roosevelt won again, as we all expected that he would. While we didn't admit this to each other or even to ourselves, we knew in our hearts that Roosevelt would not live through another term.

At about the time of this White House caucus, I have since learned, Judge Samuel Rosenman and Harold Ickes called on the President together and told him they agreed with the party leaders that a Wallace nomination would split the party wide open. If there was any doubt left in the President's mind, this probably resolved it. Ickes and Rosenman were not politicians in the sense that the rest of us were; they were primarily New Dealers. The President suggested that they go to Wallace and tell him of their fears. They did so the day after his return from China. Wallace, who seemed worn out from his journey, told them he would be willing to step aside if the President ordered him to, but not otherwise.

He then went to the White House ostensibly to report on his trip. He told the President that Harold Young had lined up 290 Convention delegates and that a forthcoming Gallup Poll would show that sixty-five per cent of Democratic voters wanted Wallace nominated again. About this time the President also told Governor Ellis Arnall of Georgia that he hoped the Georgia delegation would support Wallace. In the face of this, Roosevelt did not ask Wallace to withdraw, but on the contrary expressed the hope that it might be "the same team again" in 1944.

I went out to Chicago with Frank Walker, and we still didn't know, when we got there, whom the President finally would pick for the Vice-Presidential nomination. We thought it would be Truman, but we couldn't be sure. Roosevelt could, of course, have named anybody. All he had to do was say whom he wanted definitely and firmly. I remember a delegate from Louisiana rushing up to me after the Convention of 1940, grabbing my coat lapels, and telling me indignantly: "No one wanted Wallace—absolutely no one. Name me just one man that did." I said: "Brother, that I can do—and that one man was Roosevelt."

At that convention Bascom Timmons, a popular Washington correspondent for Texas newspapers, got the vote of one delegate for Vice-President and commented, I think correctly, that he and Wallace were in the same position—they both had one man for them.

The President was coming through Chicago on his way to the West Coast for a wartime inspection trip and wouldn't be readily available while the Convention was on. Wallace was himself an avowed candidate, and he thought he had the President's agreement at least not to interfere with the Convention's own choice. Hannegan, Pauley, and Flynn thought Roosevelt had told them to get Truman nominated, but were not positive of his support, either. Flynn tells, in his book *You're the Boss*, how Hannegan rushed up to him in Chicago with the breathless announcement: "It's all over. It's Byrnes."

The best thing Wallace had was a letter dated July 14, from Roosevelt to Senator Samuel D. Jackson of Indiana, who was scheduled to be permanent chairman of the Convention. It said in part:

... I am wholly willing to give you my own personal thought in regard to the selection of a candidate for Vice-President. I do this at this time because I expect to be away from Washington for the next few days.

The easier way of putting it is this: I have been associated with Henry Wallace during this past four years as Vice-President, for eight years earlier while he was Secretary of Agriculture, and well before that. I like him and I respect him, and he is my personal friend. For these reasons, I personally would vote for his re-nomination if I were a delegate to the Convention.

At the same time, I do not wish to appear in any way as dictating to the Convention. Obviously, the Convention will do the deciding. And it should—and I am sure it will—give great consideration to the pros and cons of its choice.

This was scarcely an all-out endorsement; yet it was closer to a public endorsement than anybody else had at the time. Newspapers that called it the "kiss of death" could have been quite wrong. It all depended upon the private instructions Roosevelt gave his political associates at the last minute.

These instructions were finally forthcoming in writing, the Saturday night before the Convention, while the President's private car stood parked in the Chicago railroad yards. Hannegan and Pauley got aboard. They asked the President for a letter they could publish reiterating what was in his penciled note to Hannegan. He wrote a letter in longhand in the presence of his two visitors and had a secretary make a typed copy for them. Hannegan put the copy in his pocket and left the Roosevelt train without reading it. When Hannegan and Pauley did read it, they found to their horror that it mentioned

Douglas as well as Truman. It was dated July 19, and said:

> You have written me about Harry Truman and Bill Douglas. I should, of course, be very glad to run with either of them and believe that either one of them would bring real strength to the ticket.

Whether Roosevelt actually thought Douglas might have a chance to blitz the Convention at this late date or only put Douglas' name in the letter to avoid the appearance of dictating a single choice to the delegates, I don't know. Hannegan and Pauley kept the contents of the letter to themselves until after Roosevelt had accepted his nomination, with the idea of leaving the Douglas supporters without enough time to take advantage of any chance the Truman-or-Douglas endorsement might give them. This delay worked as intended.

Truman took no part whatever in the maneuvers that led to his endorsement by the President. He had never discussed the Vice-Presidency with Roosevelt. In fact, he had gone to Chicago committed to Byrnes, his former colleague in the Senate, and fully prepared to deliver Byrnes' nominating speech. Truman refused to believe that he was Roosevelt's choice when first told so and was most reluctant to accept the nomination. He liked the Senate, and it represented complete fulfillment of any political ambition he had ever entertained.

It was Sidney Hillman who broke the news to him that he was to be the nominee. Truman was trying to win Hillman over to the Byrnes candidacy when the labor leader said: "Labor's first choice is Wallace. If it can't be Wallace, we have a second choice, but it isn't Byrnes."

"Who then?" Truman asked.

"I'm looking at him," said Hillman.

But Truman refused to believe even then that Roosevelt wanted him. Not only was he being difficult about it, but Byrnes and some of the favorite sons also were being sticky. Finally, to straighten out Truman, we got him into Hannegan's room at the Blackstone and literally pleaded with him to accept. Hannegan, Pauley, Walker, and I employed all the persuasive power we could muster, talking singly and in chorus. We showed him Roosevelt's original penciled note to Hannegan as well as the Truman-Douglas train letter. At that moment, Flynn quarterbacked the play. He got Roosevelt on the telephone and handed the instrument to Truman. Roosevelt personally told Truman he wanted him to be his running mate. That did it. We were all relieved to hear him say, "All right, Mr. President."

It may be interesting to note that by this time Ickes had changed his mind again and was working for Wallace. But the Kelly organization was all out for Truman, and the Convention was in its own back yard, where it could make the noise. Kelly himself probably had hoped for a deadlock into which he could slip Senator Scott

Lucas of Illinois, but he was well enough pleased with Truman. Like the other political leaders, his primary concern was to get rid of Wallace, and he threw everything he had into it. Even so, it could have been Wallace if the vote had been taken the night before it was. It could have been a stampede.

And it almost was a stampede. In spite of Kelly's best efforts, the convention hall filled up with a left-wing Wallace claque the night the Vice-Presidential balloting was scheduled to start.

The Wallaceites were equipped with banners and noisemakers. Moreover, the pipe organ played *Iowa— That's Where the Tall Corn Grows* over and over, cornier and cornier, as the hall filled. Since I was in charge of convention arrangements, I tried to find some way out of a night meeting and of silencing the organ. At last Mayor Kelly got me off the hook by proclaiming a fire hazard and thus forcing an adjournment until the following day. In the meantime, some of the favorite sons agreed to climb on the Truman bandwagon.

On the first Vice-Presidential ballot, the Convention gave Wallace 429½ votes, Truman 319½, Bankhead 98, Barkley 49½, and all others 279½. That was the uncomfortable moment.

The next time around, Truman got 1031 votes to Wallace's 105, and all others trailed hopelessly. Many delegations switched to Truman in the midst of the voting. Few realized at the time how great a victory had been won—a victory Ed Pauley and Pa Watson should have the credit for starting, and Bob Hannegan, Ed Flynn, and Frank Walker for finishing. As for me, I cherish Pauley's recollection of me as a "faithful ally" in his anti-Wallace conspiracy. Bosses are held in ill repute in the United States—and with some justice—but this was a time when the bosses saved the country's bacon.

That's all there is to the story of the Truman nomination. Roosevelt made amends to Wallace by giving him Jesse Jones' job as Secretary of Commerce. I went out campaigning with the Vice-Presidential nominee as representative of the Democratic National Committee and learned that he was much more than a Midwesterner who couldn't hurt a fly, much less a ticket. I learned that the next President of the United States would be a strong man in his own right.

CHAPTER 11

A Man
Who Won't Hurt
The Ticket

In the scheme of American politics there is nothing less important than a Vice-President unless it is a Vice-Presidential nominee. The nomination for second place on a national-party ticket is the booby prize and it is awarded for strictly negative virtues. The idea is to nominate a man who won't hurt the ticket. If he helps carry his own state, he is doing as much as anybody expects of him. Whereas the candidate for President immediately surrounds himself with advisers, speech writers, and representatives of the press, the candidate for Vice-President is fortunate if he can surround himself with anything but indifferent air. He is Throttlebottom; he has his hands full not to appear slightly ridiculous.

Harry S. Truman, after the Chicago Convention of 1944, was no exception. His position was even more insignificant than that of the usual second-place winner because he had displaced Henry A. Wallace, who had been discarded because he stood for something—something bad in the opinion of party strategists, but nevertheless something. He was the darling of the CIO. Truman, on the other hand, seemed to stand for nothing more spectacular than honesty in war contracting, which was like standing for virtue in Hollywood or adequate rainfall in the Middle West. He was nobody's darling.

After the Chicago Convention, I thought I deserved a rest, whether I needed it or not, and actually I did need it. Stage managing the show on behalf of the Democratic National Committee had been a difficult enterprise, particularly since nobody paid much attention to my directions. The job of trying to prevent the organist from playing *Iowa* at all times had been arduous in itself. Every time I strayed out of the convention hall, I was summoned back by the refrain: "That's where the tall corn grows." I left Chicago hoping never to hear that song again.

Mrs. Allen and I thought we could escape politics and the heat in Atlantic City. As it turned out, we escaped neither. The weather remained hot, and Bob Hannegan started telephoning me from New York before I could get my shirts unpacked. I avoided answering telephone calls for a while, on one pretext or another, but finally, as it usually does, my curiosity got the better of my prudence. It was Hannegan calling and would I hurry to New York. It was important. When I protested to him that I was resting and couldn't be reached for a few days, Hannegan told me a story about a justice of the peace in St. Louis.

During prohibition, it seemed, this particular justice of the peace had done very well collecting the five-dollar fees he got for handling prohibition cases. Because Hannegan had many clients involved in these cases, he had become quite a favorite of this J. P. One day when such a case was called and Bob stood up, the judge seemed disturbed. Summoning Bob to the bench, he whispered:

"Bob, are you interested in this case?"

"Yes," Bob whispered back.

"Then ask for a change of venue. I've been reached."

This same J. P., according to Hannegan, was used to receiving a long list of offenders every day with pencil marks opposite the names of those with enough political influence to be let off. One day the list was unusually long, but only two named on it were unmarked.

"Who are these two poor, friendless souls?" the judge asked. "I am forced to take judicial notice of their sad plight." Adding two pencil marks, he declared, "The court will now make it unanimous and dismiss all these cases."

Hannegan's request, and his casual reminder that that ear the Saratoga meet was being run at Belmont, convinced me that it was my duty to go to New York and find out what Hannegan had on his mind. What he had on his mind was a bad situation in Detroit, where Truman was scheduled to open his campaign on Labor Day. Arrangements had run afoul of bitter rivalry between the CIO and AF of L. If Truman made his speech to the CIO group, the AF of L would be outraged, and vice versa. Under no circumstance would the two groups sit in the same audience to hear the Vice-Presidential nominee on a ticket they were both supporting. Something had to be done about it—and quickly. So I called my friend Ed Frawley, a famous hotel man, who knows his Detroit as Joe DiMaggio knows his Yankee Stadium, and told him I wanted to have dinner with him that night. Bill Wise, an official of one of the companies with which I am associated, said he'd fly me out to Detroit in an airplane the company had just purchased. The plane behaved in an odd and alarming fashion on the way out, but Bill assured me that it wasn't the plane's fault. It was, he explained, that the ship was new and the pilot hadn't as yet learned to fly it. That was supposed to be reassuring to me. Bill never seemed to understand why it wasn't.

Frawley introduced me to all the CIO and AF of L leaders in Detroit, and I got in touch with Cy Bevan, Democratic National Committeeman for Michigan. Then ensued a week of the kind of negotiations diplomats formerly engaged in when the object was to get Chiang Kai-shek and Mao Tse-tung together in a coalition government to rule China. The deal ultimately worked out required Truman to make a speech before the CIO on the afternoon of Labor Day and another at an AF of L banquet that evening. There were other covenants as well, but I don't remember exactly what they were. There were also separate negotiations with Frank Murphy, pro-labor U. S. Supreme Court Justice from Michigan, who, being a Wallace man, didn't know whether he would grace either of the Truman meetings. As it turned out, he went to the AF of L banquet and looked impressive at the speakers' table.

Back in Washington, I was given the assignment of representing the National Committee in the Truman campaign. By this time I had seen enough of the Senator from Missouri to know that I liked him. While I had no illusions about Vice-Presidential campaigns, I did think that a Truman tour might be moderately effective. So one rainy morning Truman and Hugh Fulton, then counsel to the Truman Committee, came to my apartment at the Wardman Park to talk over arrangements. We talked about the itinerary and subject matter for speeches in considerable detail. The only thing I remember vividly about that conference was the behavior of Muggins, a blind, fourteen-year-old dog of which we were excessively fond. He was smart and temperamental. His likes and dislikes were always shown in unmistakable fashion. Certain of our friends were so cordially disliked by Muggins that he had to be banished when they came. But Muggins immediately approved of Truman. He took up a position at the Senator's feet and remained there happily throughout the talk. There was no doubt how Muggins would vote and that, somehow, reinforced my own impression of Truman.

The Senator wanted to start his tour in New Orleans before the Flood Control Congress, which he had addressed on previous occasions, so it was decided that I would go on ahead of him to California to complete arrangements for his barnstorming of the Coast. And that was the way it worked out. When I joined the Truman entourage it was installed in two Pullman cars, one occupied by Truman, Fulton, Matt Connelly, then an employee of the Truman committee, and Ed McKim, one of Truman's Nebraska friends. The other accommodated newspapermen, among them Tony Vaccaro of the Associated Press, Sam Bell of the *New York Herald Tribune*, Edward Lockett of *Time* and *Life,* Ray Lahr of UP, and Joseph Short of the *Baltimore Sun.* Others came and went, but these were the regulars.

We soon learned that Truman got up at the crack of dawn, retired early, and refreshed himself with a short nap in the middle of the day. In the intervals between rest he was a hard man to keep up with. In Washington State one day, campaigning for his old associate, Mon Wallgren, now head of the Federal Power Commission, who was then running for Governor, he made thirty speeches and ate so many heavy meals that we lost count. We got to calling the Northwest the mashed-potato circuit.

Some years later the Senate was to turn down Wall-gren's nomination, submitted by Truman, for a place on one of the important Federal boards. What the Senate seemed to hold against Wallgren, more than anything else, was his skill at billiards, probably because this skill is the classic betrayal of a misspent youth. But Truman nd Wallgren became fast friends while serving together in the Senate and they remain so to this day. Truman once asked Wallgren, who is something of a professional Scandinavian, why it was that Minnesota got all the Swedes and Missouri all the mules. "Probably," said Wallgren, "because Missouri got first choice."

In the next few weeks we covered the whole country. Truman spoke wherever the train stopped and many times at some stops. No two speeches were identical. He was at his best before a small, intimate audience. In fact, his tactics were about the same in that campaign as later in 1948, when his familiarity with the technique of the whistle-stop tour paid off handsomely. But in 1944 nobody paid much attention to the Truman effort unless he got into trouble or got out of potential trouble, as he frequently did.

I dreaded his Montana schedule because Senator Burton K. Wheeler, then violently anti-Roosevelt, was Truman's friend. Realizing by that time that one of his characteristics was loyalty to friends, I was afraid he'd be photographed telling Wheeler what a splendid fellow he was—and that this wouldn't go down very well in Washington. But when I confided my concern to Truman, he said: "Don't worry. Burt won't be there." And he wasn't. In Butte we heard Roosevelt's foreign-policy speech by radio and listened to accounts of the day he had spent driving through the streets of New York in an open car with the rain beating down. Roosevelt had counted heavily upon that demonstration of his vigor to silence reports that his health was too delicate to justify another term, and we were all interested in the outcome of the demonstration. Radio announcers covering the President's evening speech made much of the fact that many in the audience seemed to be coughing but that the President was obviously in excellent health, voice, and spirits. Vaccaro commented that "the old man evidently killed everyone else off and is himself in fine shape."

Being Frank Walker's home town, Butte was hospitality itself. Talking with his old friends, I verified one of his stories. The Socialists were strong in this mining community in the early days and once elected a mayor who, in turn, appointed an all-Socialist police force. But at the next mayoralty election, the Democrats came back into power, and their candidate, of course, appointed a Democratic chief of police. The question was what the new chief would do about the Socialist cops. When asked about his intentions, he replied: "We will give them all a fair and impartial trial and then fire the sons of bitches."

In Minneapolis, the chairman of the Truman meeting was a friend of mine, a young man named Hubert H.

Humphrey, now a Senator. When we got to Chicago, I felt the need of a rest and so remained there while Truman jaunted to Peoria, Illinois, to deliver a farm speech. I was just settling down for my rest when Jonathan Daniels called from the White House to inform me that the Hearst press was publishing a copyrighted article purporting to expose Truman as a member of the Ku Klux Klan. Jonathan was worried, and so was I.

The next morning I boarded Truman's car and, finding it filled with politicians, pushed him into the men's room, the only place available for a private conference. I told him what was happening and, at the same time, offered some advice. If it were true, I said, we'd have to say nothing and let it blow over. But if it weren't true, the only thing to do was sue Hearst. "We sue," he replied. Hugh Fulton was instructed to do so, and immediately got in touch with a libel lawyer in New York, who told us we had a case. Had the campaign been lost, the suit would have been pressed. But, as Vice-President, Truman didn't think it seemly to embroil himself in a legal argument with Hearst. The fact was, I learned later, that Truman had taken the lead in a movement to bar Kluxers from the Masonic Lodge at a time when this wasn't a politic thing to do in Missouri.

Nothing untoward happened after that until we got to Clinton, Massachusetts, where Truman was asked at a press conference what he thought of Senator David I. Walsh, another of the Roosevelt-hating isolationists. Truman said he had high hopes of winning Walsh over to the Administration's side in foreign affairs. This seemed an excellent answer to me, but it didn't go down very well with Walsh. Discussing this later with President Roosevelt and Harry Hopkins, I offered to bet them twenty dollars each that Roosevelt and Truman would carry Massachusetts by a larger majority than Roosevelt and Wallace had carried it four years earlier. Fortunately for me, they didn't take me up. Actually, Roosevelt's vote was somewhat better in 1940 than it was in 1944 in Massachusetts. But he carried the state by comfortable margins both times.

In New York, at the Madison Square Garden semi-final show of the Truman campaign, another kind of problem arose. We knew that the Communists and their sympathizers, who were Wallace's devoted friends, would be well represented, and we suspected that they would welcome an opportunity to embarrass the man who had beaten out their candidate at Chicago. Certainly the ovation for Wallace when he entered the Garden would dwarf Truman's reception. We were determined to avoid this by arranging for the two men to enter together. Senator Robert F. Wagner, who also was nervous about an incident the press could blow up on the eve of the election, supported us. So we arrived with Truman an hour in advance and kept him secluded.

We expected Wallace to show before the end of the hour, but as the time got shorter and he still didn't put in an appearance we began to suspect that he might slip through our guard. Checking up on him, we were told that he had left his hotel. Then we got a bulletin to the effect that he had forgotten his glasses and returned for them. He finally arrived one minute before the time set for the meeting to open and was taken almost literally by the forelock and marched into the huge auditorium at Truman's side. It was a great demonstration—probably for Wallace—but Truman took his bows and the publicity was all right.

While Truman proceeded via Pittsburgh and St. Louis to Independence, Missouri, to cast his vote, I returned to Washington not to vote and to catch up with my personal affairs. The affair that interested me most at the time was the success at Bowie of a two-year-old horse I owned. He had won a race and paid $125. Since I always bet twenty dollars on each of my half-mile Whirlaways when I was around, that race had cost me, because of my absence, $1250. I did a lot of complaining about that, both to Roosevelt and to Truman. But I didn't feel that I got very much sympathy, except from Harry Hopkins, who was a devoted horse player himself.

But even his sympathy was tinctured with reproach for my failure to tell him what I knew about the horse, so that he could have cashed in. I assured him that the filly hadn't told me anything, but he remained skeptical. I remember that I told him about a bookie with whom I had done business * in my early days in Washington, who later was sent for good and sufficient reason to St. Eliza-

* Note to the Kefauver Committee: my records on these transactions have been thoroughly lost.

147

beth's Hospital, a government institution handling mental patients. At St. Elizabeth's he continued to make book. But since the patients had no money, he accepted rocks as betting tokens. Every day his friends would come to him and bet five rocks on the nose on Flight Merchant in the fifth or two rocks across the board on Honeycutt in the eighth or whatever suited their fancy. The doctors were amused and pleased that the patients had found so absorbing a pastime, and the bookie was happy, too. This went on until the day when an inmate with the proclivities of a plunger rolled up a big boulder to the bookie's bench and said: "Put this on Little Elsie in the fifth at Santa Anita." The bookmaker refused. "I won't take it," he said, measuring the boulder with a shrewd eye. "You know something."

As soon as he learned that I was back in town, Roosevelt instructed Hopkins to get me to the White House that very night for dinner—just the three of us in the intimate upstairs dining room—to hash over Truman's trip. Both the President and Hopkins seemed a little tired to me that night. Nevertheless, they quizzed me closely about Truman's performance on the campaign, audience reaction and general outlook in the states we covered. I told them all I could think of, but they seemed to expect something more. Finally I told them Truman was the kind of man who appealed to me, who would appeal to them, and who would appeal to the American people. He was the kind of man who wore well. The better one knew him, the better one liked him. Roosevelt felt that

I was overoptimistic about the number of states he would carry. I got the impression that they were both eager to get the election over with so they could get on with the war.

That election came out about as expected. Truman settled inconspicuously into the Vice-Presidency. He helped Roosevelt considerably with legislation, but always behind the scenes and never ostentatiously. Like other Vice-Presidents before him, he was forgotten by most Americans until the day death made him President of the United States.

CHAPTER 12

We Just Didn't Believe It

THE Las Vegas sun was bright for April, and I was grate-fully basking in it, half asleep, when Mrs. Allen dented my reluctant consciousness with the information that Washington was calling. She had been riding, and I had started for the swimming pool, but I never got beyond the deck chair in front of our bungalow. This was the start of what was to have been a three-week vacation in Nevada, the first in a long time, and I had dozed off while speculating on the possibility of just staying in that same chair the whole three weeks.

"Find out who it is," I muttered. "Unless it's impor-tant, I'm not here."

"The operator says it's the Capitol—the Vice-President's office. She says it's important."

In the few minutes it took me to come out of my stupor and get to the telephone the connection was broken, and it took a long time to get it back. All lines to the Vice-President's office were busy. Then, when they were no longer busy, there was nobody in the Vice-President's office. That seemed strange. Room 240 in the Senate Office Building shouldn't be closed so early. It was mid-afternoon in Nevada and not yet evening in Washington.

At last I heard the voice of Shirley Green, one of the Vice-President's staff, wearily telling the Capitol operator that she would talk with Mr. Allen. Everybody else had gone to the White House. Yes, they had been trying to reach me.

"They wanted to tell you," she said, "that President Roosevelt died this afternoon at Warm Springs."

So it had come. It shouldn't have been a surprise, because some of us had half expected it. Even before the Yalta newsreels showed how tired and emaciated the President had become under the awful burden of his wartime responsibilities, Basil O'Connor had told me of his concern about the President's health. At that time I had repeated his comments to the Vice-President. Others, too, had warned Mr. Truman that the President was failing and that the Vice-President should familiarize himself with some of the affairs, particularly in the field of foreign policy and military strategy, that he would be called upon to deal with in case of the President's death.

"I just don't believe it," Truman had told me.

What he meant was that he, even more firmly than the rest of us, would not let himself believe it. We had seen Roosevelt do the impossible so often that we came to think that he was proof against the ravages of care and overwork. I am certain that neither he nor Truman considered, except as an abstraction, the possibility that the law of succession would operate before the end of the war. Had either of them thought it a real chance, Truman would have schooled himself more fully in such matters as the Teheran and Yalta agreements. It took him weeks after he entered the White House to find out about these things. He later told me that he had badly strained his eyes sitting up into the late hours with State Department documents.

One is never adequately prepared for the kind of news that came over the Washington wire that afternoon of April 12, 1945. I'm afraid I hung up the receiver before Miss Green completed her conversation. I don't remember telling Mrs. Allen the news, but I must have because she was in tears when I looked around.

"We are going home," she announced. "We are not going to stay on in this hotel where everybody hates Mr. Roosevelt."

Roosevelt was my hero, too. He had been friendly and often kind to me, but I never felt that I knew him intimately; to me, as to millions of other Americans, he was a fabulous world figure, already classified among the historic great, along with Washington and Lincoln. Yet the news of his death left me with a vacant feeling. We soon discovered that others in El Rancho Vegas, even those Mrs. Allen was thinking about when she lumped them all together as Roosevelt haters, were similarly affected. Appreciation of true greatness doesn't stop at the political barricades.

The last time I had seen Roosevelt was at a White House ceremony a few weeks before his death. In high good humor he had twitted Mrs. Allen about some ermine tails she was wearing.

"Where does George get the money for ermine?" he asked her.

"Betting on you," she answered.

Many memories of Roosevelt crowded in upon me as I tried to adjust myself to the realization that the United States and the free world had lost him—lost one of their greatest warriors before their fight was won. They would carry on without him. Already the German and Japanese fighting forces were broken. But it would be difficult to get used to the idea that the mind behind the long-jawed face would no longer be making the vital decisions. The vigor of that mind— its capacity to think and plan ahead to the next crisis, to lead public opinion along paths it wanted the people to travel, to brush aside the road blocks to achievement of the ends it conceived to be desirable—had touched every man on earth and written one of history's most exciting and eventful chapters.

Like a drowning man reviewing the events of his

life, I reviewed some of my memories of Roosevelt while awaiting full understanding of what his death meant. I had seen him in many moods, ranging from white anger to boyish delight. When I resigned as District of Columbia Commissioner, I was invited one day to take an automobile ride with him. I thought he wanted to consult me about my successor. But during a long chat about many subjects, he never mentioned the vacancy. Later I asked Marvin McIntyre why I had been invited.

"I'll tell you, George," he answered. "We had to ask you to get out of making the President ride twenty miles with a fellow who bores him to distraction. We had to have an excuse for putting off this bore. You were it. The boss didn't have anything to talk about with you, but he thought you'd be pleasant to talk about nothing with. If you see what I mean."

I saw what he meant. I was glad I hadn't insisted upon a serious discussion of District affairs. On a previous occasion I had learned the hard way that it wasn't a good idea to force the President to talk about something he didn't want to talk about. I had waited for an opening in his conversation about other things to bring up the question of votes for District of Columbia citizens. He had given me the squelching of my life. From then on, I had been a yes man in his presence. So were most of his associates, except Steve Early, his press secretary, who never hesitated to tell Roosevelt what he thought on any given subject, even if what he thought was most unpleasant to the President.

Roosevelt was always at his best while waiting to deliver a fireside chat, a chore he seemed to enjoy. Once the manuscript was ready, all arguments about it resolved, and there was nothing more to do but wait for zero hour, he liked to sit down with a few friends to a short poker game. It relaxed and entertained him. I sat in on some of those games. The President was witty and gracious, but he liked to win at poker almost as much as he did at the polls. And he was accustomed to success in both places.

He suffered defeat in only one election. That was the famous purge election campaign in which he undertook to defeat some of the Democratic Congressmen and Senators who had opposed his legislative program. All of them were re-elected over his opposition except one—Representative John O'Connor of New York. Roosevelt said he was well satisfied with that outcome. He said his feeling was like that of any good Harvard man after Harvard had lost every other game of the season but had beaten Yale.

When at Hyde Park, Roosevelt seemed quite a different man from the one who presided over the White House in Washington. There his mother, for as long as she lived, was the head of the Roosevelt household and Franklin was part boy again. She sat at the head of the table and gave the orders. Once, when I was there, Roosevelt gave me a hair-raising ride in the car especially built for him with hand levers to operate the clutch and brake. He whisked me around the estate, enjoying my nervousness and glancing at me to see if I was satisfactorily alarmed.

On that occasion I had gone with Keith Morgan to Hyde Park to present Roosevelt with the first million dollars raised by the Birthday Ball campaign for the treatment of children crippled, as he had been, by poliomyelitis. On the way to Hyde Park our car had broken down, and we had been compelled to hitchhike part of the way to get to our destination in time to keep our appointment with the President. Lots of cars passed us before one stopped, and Roosevelt later laughed heartily at the idea of two men hitchhiking with a million-dollar check in their possession.

Although capable of vindictiveness, Roosevelt was curiously detached in his attitude toward strictly political enemies. Once I listened to a speech in the Senate by Huey Long ripping Roosevelt to pieces with sarcastic fury. I described some of the Louisiana Kingfish's anti-Roosevelt histrionics to McIntyre, who insisted that I tell the President about them. Roosevelt listened fascinated. He didn't behave as one being attacked personally; there was no resentment. He was simply interested in the technique of a rival, as an actor might be interested in the performance of another actor.

On a few occasions Mrs. Allen and I were yachting guests of the President, and on one of them—a stormy week end—she became violently seasick. In the middle of the night she announced: "George, I think I'm dying."

That, I told her, would be a splendid way of attracting attention—dying on the President's yacht. The resulting anger cured her. It also amused our host when he was told about this drastic treatment for *mal de mer.*

Roosevelt's associates didn't think of him as physically handicapped any more than the public did. But his physical helplessness showed more in private and was shockingly incongruous on those occasions when one saw him being carried in the arms of a husky attendant. Ordinarily he was ingenious about using the tremendous strength in his arms and shoulders to transfer himself from his wheel chair to another chair, or vice versa. He seemed to want to conceal his handicap, even from his friends, as much as possible.

His condition never affected me much except at banquets, when he would march a long way, supporting himself on the arm of one of his sons or of an intimate friend, in time to the cadences of *Hail to the Chief.* It was painful for him to carry his heavy braces on those marches. Yet he would smile as if enjoying every step.

PART FOUR

CHAPTER 13

He Wouldn't Accept
the Party Chairmanship

My uncle John once watched Vice-President Adlai E. Stevenson crossing the lobby of the Cosmos Club in Washington during the Cleveland Administration. Turning to a group of friends, Uncle John said:

"There goes the Vice-President of the United States with nothing on his mind except the health of the President."

He meant, of course, that Stevenson was hoping that the sturdy Cleveland wasn't as well as he seemed. With the opposite implication, the same remark could have been made of Truman during his brief tenure as Vice-President. When he accepted the nomination for that office, he did so with his fingers crossed.

But no normal man, and certainly no normal politician, is completely immune from the universal human urge to power. And the White House is a magnet to which that urge, no matter how minute, must be drawn. Mr. Truman would, of course, accept the Presidency as a matter of duty and, once installed, would exercise his tremendous power with some relish, however much he might dread the responsibility.

Although I had known him only casually before his nomination, I had come to think of him as a lifelong friend. Moreover, I had come to respect his unmistakable courage, loyalty, and integrity. The wit who contrasted Roosevelt, the friend of the common man, with Truman, the common man in person, was only half right. On the surface, the President seems as common and down-to-earth as the Missouri farmer he used to be, but his heart is uncommonly stout and his head is uncommonly level. I was lucky. It wasn't as hard for me as for most Americans to get used to the idea of Truman occupying Roosevelt's place. I had known him and I knew his caliber.

It suddenly seemed to me important that I get back to Washington at once. Truman wasn't asking me to return, but I knew that he would need help getting through the confusion of the next few weeks, and Washington confusion was one of the things I had in my time helped make and therefore understood.

I soon found that reservations on regularly scheduled airlines weren't to be had on short notice. But, since I was a director of Consolidated-Vultee, it occurred to me that I might be assigned one of their planes for the trip. I telephoned Tom Girdler, chairman of the board, Harry Woodhead, the president, and everyone else I could think of, but found none of them. Finally, Harold Shaad, as assistant to the president, said he would accept the responsibility of having *Grandpappy,* the first Liberator ever turned out and and still owned by the company, pick us up at Las Vegas and take us to Washington.

The weather was bad and the trip rocky, but we arrived, without incident, at Washington Airport at one A.M., Saturday, April 14. I was glad not to know until later that our plane was reported missing for several hours while out of touch with ground radio stations en route from Las Vegas. The telephone was ringing in our apartment at the Wardman Park when we opened the door. It was Matthew Connelly, one of Mr. Truman's ablest assistants and a man of extraordinary political judgment.

"Where have you been?" he asked, fully knowing where I had been. "We're addressing Congress Monday, the armed forces Tuesday, and the San Francisco Conference the following Monday. You probably won't be much help, but you'd better get down here, anyway. See you in the morning."

The next morning, Ed Reynolds, one of my own assistants, picked me up early, and we drove to the White House, but found the front gates barred and the street choked with people. We finally parked our car and approached one of the rear gates, only to be stopped by a park policeman. Steve Early was not in the White House, he said, and as for Matt Connelly, he'd never heard of him.

"But surely you must know me," I said. "I used to be a District of Columbia Commissioner."

"Well," he replied, "I remember Hazen" (Commissioner Melvin C. Hazen, who had served with me), "but I'm danged if I remember any Allen."

That was a humiliating experience for a man who fancied himself well known in his own city. I have consoled myself since with the thought that this officer was a park policeman and therefore a subordinate of Harold Ickes. In any case, Ickes' man finally got Ed McKim on his sentry-box telephone, and McKim got us into the White House.

Connelly put us to work in the cabinet room without delay, getting together material for the three speeches he had mentioned the night before.

Later, when Truman returned from the railroad station, where he had met the Roosevelt funeral train, he came to the cabinet room with personal instructions. His speech to Congress, which would be his first public statement as President, he said, would emphasize two things: first, that he intended to go down the line on President Roosevelt's policies and, second, that Roosevelt's unconditional-surrender terms to Germany and Japan would stand. Afterward, there was some discussion about the advisability of sticking to the unconditional-surrender ultimatum. The argument was made that this policy was being turned to propaganda uses by Goebbels and should be abandoned. Truman, in his first major policy decision, refused to soften the Roosevelt-Churchill line.

We worked the rest of the day in the cabinet room, in the main stream of traffic to and from the President's office, and then transferred operations to the Roosevelt funeral train. Truman was busy assuring Roosevelt cabinet members that he needed their co-operation, at least temporarily, and gathering up the reins of government where his predecessor had dropped them.

It wasn't until after the funeral, on Sunday, that Matt and I had another chance to discuss the speech to Congress with the President. He liked the material we had prepared, made some suggestions, and then proposed that we go over the text with former Supreme Court Justice James Byrnes. After reading our draft, Byrnes outraged my pride of authorship with the remark that he, too, had trouble putting his thoughts on paper. At one of the stops en route from Hyde Park to Washington reporters walked back along the platform and apparently saw me with the manuscript in my hand. As a result, I was soon reading newspaper stories to the effect that I was Mr. Truman's speech writer.

At the President's suggestion, I didn't bother to deny it. At the same time, I had a discussion with Jonathan Daniels, who had been one of Mr. Roosevelt's secretaries, about the form of address. Ordinarily, when a President appears before Congress, he includes the Vice-President among those specifically saluted. Daniels said he would look up the protocol when we got back to Washington—that it was a matter of no great importance in any case.

"This is more important than you think, Jonathan," I told him. "We must get this salutation right. So far, that's about all there is to the speech."

It should be explained, perhaps, how a Presidential address is written. Like all recent occupants of the White House, Truman is much too busy for personal research and composition. So he has adopted the customary practice of outlining to assistants in a general way what he wants to say and then, when they have reduced his generalizations to specific language, editing the result. Almost every Presidential speech represents a group effort, yet it is, in the end, the President's own.

First drafts of Mr. Truman's speeches are always triple-spaced by White House typists to allow room for his own corrections and interlineations. Often these original manuscripts contain more longhand additions and deletions than typewritten lines by the time the President is through with them. I assisted on the first three speeches delivered by President Truman. Later Judge Samuel Rosenman, who had worked on Mr. Roosevelt's speeches and state papers, agreed to do the same thing temporarily for Truman. Eventually, members of the permanent White House staff did the speech work as a matter of routine. Clark Clifford, a brilliant young lawyer and the President's former counsel, did most of the speech work up to the time of his retirement.

Those early days in the White House were wild and woolly. Truman knew the United States government and the duties of the Presidency. He agreeably surprised the press and the country with his grasp, his energy, and his decisiveness. He deliberately played the part of the emphatic chief of a great state—overplayed it at times, perhaps—to make it clear to the world that President Roosevelt's death would mean no lessening of U. S. pressure on the Germans and the Japanese.

Sometimes he answered questions too quickly and certainly at press conferences; later he learned to be more cautious, as any President must. The surprising thing is that he made so few mistakes in those first weeks. What saved him from serious trouble was his political experience and excellent political position. Coming from a border state, he was neither a Northerner nor a Southerner. Although he had a down-the-line New Deal, pro-labor voting record, he was not classified in the public mind as a New Dealer of the extremist Wallace school. Thus, he was acceptable both to Northern labor and to orthodox Southern Democrats.

Truman's unique position in the party was recognized as early as 1943 by some of the party's leaders. It is a little-known fact that he was offered the chairmanship of the Democratic National Committee that year. Frank C. Walker, then chairman of the Committee, was eager to retire. Casting about for new leadership, he did his best to persuade Truman to take the job, but Truman declined, wisely deciding that his war investigations were too important to give up. Had he accepted, the entire course of American history would have been changed.

White House employees should have a union to look out for their wages and working conditions, both of which are deplorable. I worked in the executive offices without a desk for weeks after Truman's swearing in and for months without a salary. I might as well have been in a slave-labor camp. I dropped out of sight one day and nobody heard from me or knew what had become of me. When my friends inquired, my wife told them I seemed to have a job down in a nice, cool, air-conditioned building on Pennsylvania Avenue, but just what I was doing there she didn't know. At times, I didn't know either.

In fact, I don't know yet just how I happened to go to work in the White House. It was my idea that I would try to make myself useful for a few days or a few weeks at the most, helping the President as best I could. I knew hundreds of people in the executive departments and in Congress. True, I was better informed about the kind of golf or poker they played than about the kind of work they did, but even my kind of knowledge might be of some use. The Home Insurance Company could worry along without me for a while.

The worst part of my employment was getting up with the birds to be at the White House for Truman's first morning staff conference, which took place at the hour when I ordinarily started turning over for another cat nap. The sleepy group that gathered in the President's office for these dawn conferences included at the start

Matt Connelly, who had been on Truman's investigating committee staff, General Harry Vaughan, Truman's Military Aide, Charlie Ross, a schoolmate of Truman and for years a Washington correspondent and editorial writer for the *St. Louis Post-Dispatch*, Sam Rosenman, Commodore Jake Vardaman, Naval Aide and former St. Louis banker, and me. A little later, John Steelman joined this group and is still one of the President's most effective aides. The President kept on his desk a permanent file with compartments marked with the names of each of his assistants, and he stuffed into these compartments letters to be answered, notes ordering some chore done, and instructions of all kinds.

Presently, I noticed that there was a compartment marked "George Allen," and that is how I knew I was working there. My compartment soon filled up with the names of men Truman thought he might use in his Cabinet and other parts of his Administration. It was my duty to find out whether they could fill the jobs he had in mind for them, whether they would consent to do so, and to arrange for their appointments.

My files were kept in my pockets, and my work was done anywhere I could find a free telephone—mostly in the cabinet room. Finally, I got the executive offices so cluttered up with handfuls of papers and notes that Matt Connelly moved me into an office of my own in the old State Department building across the street from the executive wing of the White House, where several of the President's assistants already occupied space.

My office had once been used by Secretary of War Newton D. Baker. Even if I didn't have a job or a title, I figured that Lieutenant Allen, of the First World War, had
somehow jumped a lot of grades to be sitting in the Secretary's office, and that happy thought helped my morale.
The fact was that I couldn't afford to accept a government salary or title. I remained on the payroll of the
Home Insurance Company at a considerably higher figure than Truman could have paid me. Moreover, I'd had
enough of paid government service in the District Commissionership and didn't want any more of it.

I kept telling myself that I'd go back to tending my
own business in a few days, anyway. But as the weeks
stretched into months and the months into a year and I
got in the habit of exercising great authority in the name
of the President, I couldn't find the right moment to tell
Truman that he'd have to struggle along without me,
difficult as I thought that might be.

Truman's first three important public statements were
a speech to Congress, another to the armed forces, and
still another opening the San Francisco meeting of the
United Nations—the meeting at which the new world
organization was launched. After getting through the first
three, the President started preparing for the fourth—
a speech closing the San Francisco meeting, which he was
to deliver in person.

At that time, great hopes were held out for the United
Nations. It had not yet become apparent, as it did later,
that Soviet Russia had no intention of co-operating in a

spirit of give-and-take with its Second World War allies. There had been intimations of its intransigence before this, but it took a long time for the rest of the world to learn that Joseph Stalin was out to destroy capitalism and democracy everywhere and by whatever means came to hand. On a week-end trip down the Potomac on the President's yacht, it was decided that I should go to San Francisco in advance and make arrangements for his appearance.

As soon as I arrived in San Francisco, I discovered that there was sharp disagreement over the proper setting for the President's speech. The State Department was taking the position that Truman should speak to the United Nations delegates in the Opera House, where the United Nations charter had been drawn up and adopted. Truman's political friends, on the other hand, wanted to move the closing session to a large auditorium where San Franciscans, as well as their guests from abroad, could hear and see him. I sided with the State Department, feeling that the speech would be more effective in the same setting as the charter deliberations, and it was finally delivered in the Opera House.

I flew to San Francisco by State Department plane and was met by Jim Rowley of the Secret Service, then one of the White House detail under George Drescher but now chief of the detail. We had no sooner reached the Fairmont Hotel than I was informed that the White House was calling from Washington with an urgent message. It was the President calling me. He wanted to know whether

I was alone and could talk confidentially. I said I could. Then he proposed that I sound out Secretary of State Edward Stettinius about resigning. Truman wanted to appoint his old friend James Byrnes Secretary of State but also wanted to keep Stettinius in the public service—perhaps somewhere in the new United Nations organization. I hung up the telephone, bursting with this confidence, only to be confronted by a State Department stenographer with a transcript of my conversation with the President. I asked her to forget about the transcript, which I assume she did.

Breaking the news to the Secretary of State that he wasn't going to be Secretary of State much longer was an assignment in diplomacy for which my experience, varied as it was, hadn't equipped me. I considered various approaches to Stettinius and finally decided upon the direct announcement. I told him that Truman naturally wanted a Secretary of State he could call his own, much as he esteemed Stettinius, that his successor would be Jimmie Byrnes, and that his resignation was desired.

Stettinius was inclined to be a little bitter about it and to attribute his undoing to the machinations of Democratic politicians. Nor did my assurance that Truman felt he might be even more useful heading the United States delegation to the UN assuage his hurt. This, he said, would not be a sufficiently important assignment to utilize the experience of a former Secretary of State. But after talking it over with Dr. Isaiah Bowman, of Johns Hopkins University, one of his closest friends, Stettinius decided to resign the secretaryship and accept the UN appointment. We worked together over his letter of resignation for several days before achieving a satisfactory draft.

He turned out to be a good loser, which is the ultimate test of the gentleman. Back in Washington, I received a letter from him: "Dear George: I want to send you this personal note," it said, "to express again my deep appreciation of the frankness and friendliness which you displayed in connection with my resignation as Secretary of State and my prospective nomination as representative of the United States to the United Nations. Ed."

With Stettinius no longer a problem, I flew to Olympia, Washington, to report to the President, who was spending a few days relaxing with Governor Mon Wallgren, a former Senate colleague. He was satisfied with the Stettinius letter, a copy of which I had in my pocket at that time.

Back in San Francisco, I decided to learn something about the mechanics of the new United Nations organization and attended some of the Big Five meetings as a guest of Stettinius.

It was hard to follow the deliberations of the United States, British, Russian, Chinese, and French representatives, however, without knowing the background of the deliberations. So I asked Stettinius if he could get some State Department attaché, who was familiar with the preliminary negotiations, to give me a fill-in. That very day he sent around to my room a personable, bright, obviously well-informed young man to tell me about the UN organization, its origins at the Yalta Conference, and its probable setup. He briefed me for several hours, using simple language and treating me quite properly as an eighth-grader in my knowledge of diplomacy.

When he was through he asked me whether I had a copy of the speech President Truman would deliver at the close of the San Francisco meeting. When I said I had, he asked whether he might borrow a copy to read at his leisure and return. He did return it in due course with the comment that he considered it excellent. He was extremely curious as to who had assisted in the preparation of the material. The young man's name was Alger Hiss.

When it was all over at San Francisco, I shared the hopes of others that this latest version of the League of Nations might at last establish something approaching world law and eventually outlaw war. But I was skeptical. The veto power retained by each of the big nations didn't bode well for the future of the United Nations. Unless the members sacrificed some of their sovereignty, it seemed to me then that the UN would not survive a real world crisis any better than the League did. Moreover, it was becoming apparent by this time that the Russians were going to be troublemakers on a grand scale. Truman was finding out what Roosevelt knew shortly before his death, after he experienced the disillusion stemming from Russian conduct in Poland—that the Soviet Union's word wasn't worth the paper it was written on and the red tape to tie it up. Even so, Truman remained hopeful that relations with the Soviet Union could be improved.

I returned East from San Francisco with Truman and his party, stopping off en route at Salt Lake City. Here the Truman entourage was so new at its job that the simplest kind of arrangement became complicated and confused. One of the aides was so out of temper that he got to mumbling to himself in the presence of others. Vaughan observed that he didn't mind listening to this fellow talking to himself but would get worried if he started sassing himself back. From Salt Lake we went on to Independence, Missouri, Truman's home town, where he delivered an informal speech to a capacity crowd at the local Mormon Tabernacle. He commented that he had been speaking in that hall for years but never before had been able to fill it.

After a press conference, Truman beckoned me to his car and we drove off together to near-by Grandview for a call on his aged mother. Small, bent, and peppery, she was the very personification of the pioneer American woman. "Mama, did you hear me speak last night?" Truman asked. She answered that she had. "What did you think of it?" he persisted. She said, "You were pretty good."

He introduced me as a Mississippi Democrat and added that I claimed never to have seen a Republican until I was twelve years old. Mrs. Truman commented: "He didn't miss much."

Back in Washington, the President started reorganizing the Roosevelt Administration—making it over to suit his own purposes. Several of the Roosevelt Cabinet officers resigned—some with good grace and some with bad.

Frances Perkins was the first and the most gracious. She realized that the new President would have to surround himself with his own people.

Henry Morgenthau, Jr., kept wanting Truman to give him some guarantee as to status and tenure. One day he put his desires in the form of a demand and left the White House assured of becoming an ex-Secretary of Treasury.

Harold Ickes was a habitual resigner. His friend, Budget Director Harold D. Smith, once told me that Ickes had resigned about fifteen times during the Roosevelt Administrations but had always been persuaded to reconsider. But when he resigned to Truman, his resignation was promptly accepted. I was reminded of the epitaph I once saw on a tombstone in Oklahoma: "He kept asking for it until he got it."

With the work of reorganization still incomplete, the President interrupted it to attend the Big Four Conference at Potsdam. He at first planned to take with him both Jim Byrnes, by now the Secretary of State, and Fred M. Vinson, still the Economic Stabilizer although already picked for Secretary of Treasury.

Bags were packed and sent to the ship before somebody awoke to the realization that if the ship were sunk and both Truman and Byrnes drowned, Morgenthau would become President of the United States. There being no

Vice-President, he would succeed to the Presidency as the senior living Cabinet member.

So Vinson's bags were quietly retrieved and he was appointed Secretary of Treasury before Truman and Byrnes departed. Thus, Vinson would have succeeded to the Presidency in case of fatal accident to both the President and the Secretary of State. Later, of course, Truman encouraged Congress to change the succession law in such a way that the Speaker of the House would become President if both the President and the Vice-President died or were incapacitated.

At Potsdam, the President got more education about the ways and wiles of the Russians. His old friend, Ed Pauley, then serving as Reparations Commissioner with the rank of Ambassador, had spent a long time in Russia preparing for the Potsdam Conference and was on hand to tell the President what he had learned.

He was able to prove by photographs taken just before the conference that the Russians were looting Germany in violation of every commitment they had made about reparation payments. Stalin, it developed, wanted to talk about nothing but the termination of Lend-Lease, which had outraged him, and about how much machinery and goods he could get out of Germany and Austria. He even professed to be uninterested in the atomic bomb or unable to understand what it was when Truman told him the United States was about to use it on Japan. From what we have learned since about Russian espionage, it is now apparent that he knew as much—and perhaps more —about the United States' atomic-bomb development as the President did.

While the President was abroad, I transacted some personal business for him. The afternoon he left he asked me to check up on the state of his insurance policies, which were in a safety-deposit box in one of the Washington banks, and I, of course, said I would if I could get at them. There wouldn't be time for him to get them himself, so he gave me a handwritten note to Josh Evans, vice-president of the Hamilton National Bank. It said: "Dear Mr. Evans: Please allow Mr. George Allen to take my life-insurance policies out of my safe-deposit box. Sincerely, Harry Truman. P.S. He has my key."

There was beginning to be talk at that time about the "Missouri gang" and Truman's connection with the Pendergast machine. It occurred to me then that a politician who was not afraid to let an associate go through the contents of his safe-deposit box surely did not have much to hide.

It was not easy for Truman to get the hang of the Presidency, probably the world's most exacting job. He was a friendly man who loved his family, his companions, and the routine of his quiet life. He had always been a hard worker and therefore wasn't bothered too much by the grinding drudgery of the Presidency. But he missed the easy camaraderie of the Capitol and the Senate. He changed his ways as little as possible after entering the White House. He continued to rise early, take a morning walk, and breakfast before going to his office at eight A.M. He continued to take a daily nap after lunch. He then worked the rest of the afternoon, but sometimes swam in the White House pool before dinner. In the evening he often continued to work, but sometimes read his beloved history books—his favorites being accounts of the American Civil War.

Except for the fact that Truman was in his late fifties then, and is sixty-six now, I can see no difference between the Senator and the President. The setting is so different, though, that it is now harder to see the real man.

Harry Truman is superlatively normal, both physically and mentally. He eats and drinks what he pleases because his stomach is always in good order, and his stomach is always in good order because it never pleases him to eat or drink excessively. His mind is the same kind of organ; it works normally, and the result is that it makes common sense. Just as his stomach doesn't need pills, so his mind doesn't need nostrums. If the mind could be tested, as blood pressure is tested, Truman's would be precisely normal. There are no odd and unpredictable quirks to his personality.

Everyone has a few friends he likes to run into on a street corner. These people have a quality that defies definition. One feels better for talking with them and seeing them, regardless of what they say. One is somehow bucked up by them. Truman is such a person. He gives his friends more than he takes from them. I don't know exactly why, but I think it is because he has infectious courage. I have never seen him in a despairing mood, although I have seen him suffer defeats that would plunge me into depths—in fact, have.

He never loses hope or, better than that, faith that the worst situation will right itself.

It is this side of his character, I believe, that makes him better than an adequate President. The Presidency of the United States is, in its nature, one of the world's loneliest jobs. It is the loneliness of a stranger in a crowd. The President has too much power to have really close friends; nobody he deals with, outside his immediate family, is wholly disinterested—completely unconscious of the overwhelming fact that this man holds the world's biggest job. This loneliness can and has broken strong Presidents. But it will never break Harry Truman.

Resistance to loneliness, which is a facet of his courage, is probably one of his best pieces of Presidential equipment. He must have learned the art of being alone with himself when he was a farm boy. He certainly practiced it as the Baptist captain of a battery of tough Irish gunners in the First World War. He practiced it again when his business failed and through his years on the bench and in politics, scrimping to pay off debts he felt morally bound to settle, even though they were legally uncollectable. And again, when he decided to use the atom bomb, when he fired Henry Wallace, when he clamped down on John L. Lewis, when he determined to win re-election even though everyone else thought it impossible, and when he ordered American troops to the defense of South Korea.

Many Americans who used to be skeptical of Truman's capacities have now come to recognize and admire his tough courage. But some of these same Americans remain unconvinced that his statesmanship measures up to the standard set by Roosevelt. The doubters are forever looking over and around Truman for the advisers they think must be responsible for his assured policy-making in times of crisis. "I wonder who really thought that out," they say. "Acheson? Vinson? Barkley?"

Here are some facts these questioners might think over: There is not now in Truman's Cabinet a single man who was there when he took over the Presidency, yet there has been no essential change in his domestic policies since he took the oath of office. Dean Acheson is Truman's fourth Secretary of State (following Stettinius, Byrnes, and General George Marshall), yet there has been no turn in the Administration's foreign-policy line since the end of the Second World War. The conclusion to be drawn from these facts is obvious: Truman is his own boss; he listens to advisers, but none of them is or ever has been his Svengali.

I have not always agreed with Truman's policies, but I have never doubted that they were his, nor have I ever made the mistake of trying to talk him out of them. Once his mind is made up, he is stubborn. But his stubbornness is not bullheadedness. He is as unfailingly thoughtful of those who disagree with him as of those who agree.

Before I retired from politics, while I was still a part of the Truman Administration, I was convinced that one of my functions was to give the President surcease occasionally through laughter. But now that it is all over, I can admit the truth: that he cheered me up more often than I cheered him.

Americans sometimes forget what a difficult task their chief executive performs. No matter how tired he gets, he can't rest except in short takes. No matter how discouraged he becomes, he can't resign. There's no one to resign to. No matter how lonely he gets, there's nobody he can confide in completely. He lives in a goldfish bowl almost devoid of privacy. Yet Harry Truman appeared to thrive on it from the beginning, and I think he has been helped more than most people can possibly realize by an understanding wife and a wonderful daughter.

Unlike the President, I soon withered under the heat that too often focused on my little corner of the executive offices. I got to reaching for the morning paper with an apprehensive hand, wondering what the day's troubles would be. Any trouble, anywhere in the world, more often than not becomes the trouble of the President and his assistants. I soon wanted out.

CHAPTER 14

One Enchanted Political Career

I LIKE to think of Alben Barkley as the very model of a modern American politician. He's one of the best and most indefatigable conversationalists I know. Conversation being my favorite sport, he has been over the years one of my favorite friends. He has humorous intelligence, rugged integrity, and durable ingenuity. Even the Vice-Presidency hasn't submerged him. Any Vice-President who can make the country remember his name and face well enough to keep his identity from becoming a catch question in the radio quiz programs a few weeks after election day is no ordinary man.

Barkley not only has done this, but he has done it in the most delightful way imaginable—by becoming, at seventy-two, the hero of a romance the country followed avidly through its long-distance Washington-to-St. Louis courtship and its satisfactory denouement in his marriage to Mrs. Jane Hadley. And the bride has turned out to be so gracious that even the Washington felines, who are among the world's cattiest, can't lay a claw on her. The Barkleys have made a reality of the *South Pacific* idyl.

Barkley, before he got the job, used to tell a story illustrating his opinion of the second highest office the American people can bestow. "There once was a farmer who had two sons," the story went. "Both boys showed great promise in early life. But the elder son went to sea and the younger son was elected Vice-President and neither has ever been heard from since." He has now stopped telling this story.

Long before he became Vice-President and a bridegroom, Barkley had lived several full lives, some tragic, some happy. He had proved that he could take them as they came, laughing or snapping his fingers in fortune's face, as the script indicated. His are the qualities that make successful politicians; lack of them is what breaks most aspirants for the life political.

Sometimes these qualities are held in low esteem by the critics of American politics. They are virtues too florid for their taste. But that is only because the critics are so often pallid themselves. It is easy for the nonparticipant to look down his own nose at the performer whose nose is being broken in the melee and then to proclaim a distaste for broken noses. To me a politician doesn't look right until his nose has been flattened a few times. The way Barkley looks is the way a politician should look. He has been battered into the mellow but still tough state of graceful wisdom that becomes the career politico.

It is sometimes proclaimed in stentorian tones that ours is a government of laws, not men. But anyone who has ever dealt with the actualities, as distinct from the theories, of American government recognizes this as eyewash. Men make our laws; men administer them. The laws are imperfect because they are made by imperfect men; these imperfect laws are imperfectly administered because other imperfect men read them and apply them to specific situations.

Like every other government the world has ever seen, ours is a government of men. Over the years we have been fortunate in finding good men and occasionally wise men to make and administer our laws. There have been, it is true, a few scoundrels and a few fools among our leaders. There are a few of this variety, no doubt, in present-day Washington. But not many.

The law may not be, as a Dickens character put it, "a fool, a ass," but neither is it an omniscient design imposed upon us worldlings by some unworldly force. In the last analysis the Supreme Court says what it is and the Supreme Court, too, is made up of fallible men who frequently change their minds. Operating within the law, the late Huey Long was able to build up what looked suspiciously like a dictatorship in Louisiana.

I have heard it said of Montana that it is a great state—a place where a man can do anything he's big enough to do. So it is with American law. Men can do with it anything they're big enough to do. And the place where they can do the most with it is in the United States Senate. Unlike the House of Representatives, which is so populous that men lose themselves in it, the Senate is small enough for any one of the ninety-six members to distinguish himself—and to leave an imprint on his times—if he has something to print.

During Roosevelt's second term, after Barkley had succeeded Joseph Robinson as majority leader of the Senate, I followed the Kentucky Senator's career with more than casual interest. Since he had beaten my friend, Pat Harrison, for the leadership, my inclination was to hope that he would botch the job. But I simply couldn't do it. Barkley was too thoroughly graceful a winner and too effective a statesman to be wished ill by me or anyone else who was at all in sympathy with the Roosevelt program he was engineering through the Senate.

It was the fashion in those days, particularly among enemies of the New Deal, who were many and powerful, to sneer at "Dear Alben"—a tag fixed on him by the letter Roosevelt wrote endorsing him for the leadership over Harrison. He was said to be a wheel horse, which he of course was. But it was generally assumed that he pulled whatever Roosevelt gave him to pull, whether he liked it or not, and this was never so. Barkley pulled the Roosevelt load because he thoroughly believed in the bulk of the Roosevelt program. When he didn't believe, he didn't pull. And when he wasn't pulling, he let Roosevelt know it.

Through that period, moreover, Barkley was sitting up nights with his sick wife, an invalid during the last five years of her life, or traveling by airplane to fill speaking engagements—engagements he had to take to supplement his Senatorial income enough to meet doctor bills and other family expenses. He frequently went to the Senate floor sleepless to face a killing day of debate and cloak-room wangling. I came to think of him in those times— and so did most of his friends—as a sort of modern-day saint.

Barkley came in for more abuse during the campaign of 1938, when he was opposed by A. B. (Happy) Chandler, later to become the czar of baseball, for the Democratic Senatorial nomination. It was said that Barkley and Harry Hopkins were using relief funds for political purposes. But the relief was necessary and if its recipients displayed their gratitude for Federal help by supporting the Administration in power, history should give Barkley and Hopkins absolution.

I couldn't do much for Barkley in his campaign except hope for him. I probably should not have done even that because in 1938 Chandler, then Governor of Kentucky, had made me Commanding General of the Kentucky Colonels, a very great honor, which I appreciated. While the appointment didn't convince me that Chandler, who later went to the Senate as Barkley's colleague, was the greatest statesman of all time, neither was I the greatest Commanding General of Kentucky Colonels. The Kentucky Colonels are a big army for any one man to command, and the United States Senate is a big place in which to distinguish oneself. Chandler was an able Senator and is, whatever the sports writers say, an effective Baseball Commissioner.

By 1944, Roosevelt had got in the bad habit of taking Barkley for granted. He seemed to believe the press' contention that his majority leader was his rubber stamp. The result was that when Roosevelt vetoed a tax bill Barkley had broken his back carrying through the Senate, the majority leader denounced the veto on the floor and then resigned the leadership. Senate Democrats, with Roosevelt's approval, immediately re-elected him. But Roosevelt never quite forgave this defection.

That doubtless was one of the reasons Roosevelt turned thumbs down on Barkley for the Vice-Presidential nomination in 1944, although age was the reason he gave. Even Truman, who always entertained the highest regard for Barkley, his own former leader in the Senate, offered the Vice-Presidential nomination to Supreme Court Justice William O. Douglas before approving Barkley's nomination as his running mate in 1948. Barkley naturally resented this a little, complaining that he had been offered a hot biscuit only after it had been passed around long enough to get cold. But when some of his friends suggested to Barkley that he challenge Truman for the Presidential nomination, the Senator replied: "I'd rather be loyal than President."

If politicians had a heaven, this statement would be enough in itself to assure Barkley a place next to the throne on the right-hand side. Loyalty is a fetish with politicians, and political loyalty is a special kind of virtue. It isn't like loyalty to school, home, or even country. It has its own set of rules, disciplines, and dispensations.

As practiced in politics, loyalty isn't always strictly reciprocal and isn't expected to be. The higher a politician rises in the hierarchy, the stricter the loyalty he is entitled to receive from his subordinates and the more relaxed the loyalty he is expected to give them in return. There are good reasons for this, and all veteran politicians—or almost all—recognize them. Those who don't become embittered.

A President or a governor or a mayor—the chief executive of any unit of government to a greater or less degree —occupies a terribly vulnerable position. The hazards to which he is exposed are the sum total of all the errors and all the temptations to which all his subordinates are exposed. If any one of his subordinates lets him down, his whole house of cards may fall and, with it, the fortunes and futures of all his associates.

Thus a top leader, out of loyalty to his whole organization, may be justified, under the rules of the game as it is played, in disloyally throwing one or two subordinates to the wolves. President Roosevelt hated to dump a subordinate, but he sometimes did it for what he considered the good of his Administration, or the necessity of appeasing his critics, or both. He did it when he consented to the substitution of Truman for Wallace at the Chicago Convention in 1944. While this might have been regarded as disloyalty to Wallace in any other pursuit, in politics it was a justified act of loyalty to Roosevelt's other associates, who might have been thrown out of office had Wallace proved as much of a handicap to the ticket as they thought he would.

Truman is inordinately respected by his political associates because he regards loyalty, in spite of his exalted position, as a two-way street. He gives as much as he expects to get. He fired Wallace out of his Cabinet, to be sure, but only under extraordinary provocation. Moreover, Wallace was not a member of the President's own political family; he was a Roosevelt legacy. Truman refused to repudiate Tom Pendergast, the Kansas City political boss, even after the boss had gone to jail; he has even shouldered on occasion full responsibility for odds and ends of "red herring" left over from his predecessor's management—this out of a quixotic kind of loyalty to the memory of Roosevelt.

All this may count against Truman with nonpoliticians, but it endears him to the political fraternity as nothing else can. And this is understandable. In a field of activity where the outs are forever on the hunt for some way of getting in, the ins must herd together for mutual protection, rumps together and horns presented to the would-be intruders. And this is more than just a matter of self-preservation.

If members of a party believe in the principles for which their party stands—as both Democrats and Republicans can be assumed to do—then these principles are worthy of group defense with any legitimate weapon and by use of any fair tactic. Patronage, for example, is one of the legitimate weapons, and its use can be defended on the ground that it gives the ins only a reasonable house percentage. With all their troubles and responsibilities, they have it coming to them.

In politics one frequently hears it said that so-and-so may be an s.o.b. but he is our s.o.b. and therefore deserving of our support. Recently one of my party's candidates for high office was asked by a heckler at a political meeting: "What about Formosa?" He shouted back in a voice bristling defiance: "I'll carry it by two hundred votes." But I won't name him, because he's our man and I hope he beats their man, even though their man probably knows all about Formosa.

Once the nominations had been made and the 1948 Convention was over, everybody concerned was completely reconciled. Leslie Biffle, Secretary of the Senate, one of Truman's close friends and most effective political collaborators, had supported Barkley openly through the uncertain period of Truman's attempt to induce Douglas to accept the Vice-Presidential nomination, but this disagreement between the President and his right-hand man in the Capitol didn't make the slightest difference in their subsequent relations. Wounds suffered in the course of the convention quickly healed, leaving not a vestige of a scar. Barkley plunged into the campaign with all his incomparable vigor and has been a source of strength to Truman ever since.

Another Kentuckian, Chief Justice of the United States Fred M. Vinson, likewise has made an enormous contribution to the Truman Administration, first as War Mobilizer, then as Secretary of the Treasury, and finally as successor to Chief Justice Harlan Stone. Not only has Vinson had a stabilizing effect on the Supreme Court, but he has been a valued personal adviser and friend to the President. These men who have been through the Kentucky political mill seem to have a particularly keen understanding of the American voter and the American system. And loyalty to the Democratic party comes to them as naturally as eating. Vinson tells how his father, expressing his passionate devotion to the party, bet a $120 mule on Cleveland to beat Harrison in 1888 three days after it was definitely known, even in Kentucky, that Harrison had won the election.

Barkley manages to be both a realist and an idealist. Some of his best political stories illustrate his understanding of political behaviorism. One of them, which has become a classic, concerns a constituent whom he counted upon for active help in a campaign only to find that the help wasn't forthcoming. "I took this fellow to task," Barkley relates. " 'Didn't I appoint your son postmaster?' I asked him. He admitted that I had. 'Didn't I send your nephew to West Point?' Again he conceded that I had. 'Didn't I get your brother out of that tax trouble he was in?' He acknowledged that I did. 'Then why are you letting me down in this campaign?' I demanded. He answered: 'It is true that you did all these things for me, and I appreciated them, but what have you done for me lately?' "

It is, of course, a political truism that gratitude, to the politician, is thankfulness for favors about to be received.

Talking about his own troubles, Barkley likes to compare himself with a hound dog belonging to a farmer who used to live ten miles out of Paducah. The farmer brought the hound to town regularly on Saturday nights and left the dog outside the saloon where the master himself tanked up for the week. Just as regularly, the town kids tied tin cans to the hound's tail. Finally, as Barkley tells it, the dog got so accustomed to this maltreatment that he backed up to every pile of tin cans he saw.

For all his disillusionments about men, and particularly politicians, Barkley is still deeply devoted to many causes sponsored by good-willers of all kinds. He is an ardent supporter of Truman's civil-rights program, for example. His resentment of unequal rights for Negroes is illustrated by the story of the Negro who tried to join a fashionable city church. When the congregation turned him down, he appealed to the minister, who, in turn, suggested that he take his troubles directly to the Almighty in prayer. Some time after he had received this advice, the Negro and the clergyman met on the street. Asked how he had made out, the Negro replied: "I told the Lord I was afraid I wasn't going to get to be a member of this church, and He said to me, 'Don't you worry about that. I've been trying for twenty years to get into that church and I haven't made it yet.' "

Another Barkley story, illustrative of nothing in particular, is about a lady who walked into a bookstore and asked the clerk what he had in stock that might interest her. Picking up the volume closest to his hand, the clerk said: "Here's a very interesting book called *The Kentucky Cardinal.*" "I'm not interested in Catholic books," she said. "But, madam," the clerk persisted, "this cardinal is a bird." Impatiently the lady said: "I don't care what he is; I'm still not going to read a Catholic book."

His friend Bob Hope is probably a better storyteller than Barkley, but I don't think offhand of anyone else who is. Senator Robert Taft is probably a more profound student of national problems, but few, if any, other members of the Senate are. No Vice-President since Tom Marshall, who made himself famous by saying, "What this country needs is a good five-cent cigar," has been as well known and well loved as Barkley. With the possible exception of Ezio Pinza, no man of Barkley's full maturity has become a romantic public figure in our time.

But beyond all this, measured by my own favorite yardstick that "a man is as big as the things that annoy him," Barkley is a very big man indeed. America could use more like him.

CHAPTER 15

Not Center Fielder
for the Chicago Cubs

WHY any sane man knowingly and willfully enters the service of the United States government in a conspicuous capacity if he has any other reasonably honest way of making a living is to me an insoluble mystery. Why I did it— I, of all people—can be explained only as a temporary lapse from sanity.

I must have been off my rocker the morning President Truman asked me to remain behind in his office after the breakup of the regular morning staff conference.

"George," he said, "I want you to do something for me. I want you to go over to the RFC for a year. I have nobody there and I think I should have. Will you do this for me?"

I said yes, of course, and I've been making up the speeches I should have delivered ever since. I should have said: "Mr. President, how can you ask such a thing?" Or I should have said: "Mr. President, who do you think you are, the President of the United States?" Or, at the very least, I should have said: "Mr. President, I like you. I know you have a hard time getting men to accept the hideous hazards of public service. But you and I are friends. Why pick on me? Let's load this onto one of our enemies —somebody we both hate, somebody who has this punishment coming to him."

I not only said none of these things, but I actually was fatuous enough to be pleased. The RFC—the Reconstruction Finance Corporation—was the government's big lending agency, the biggest bank in the world. Here was a place where I could put to good use my experience in business and what I liked to think of as my common sense about the kind of business that deserved help from the government. Here I could be of real service both to the President and to the country, or so I thought.

Until then, remember, I had been serving the President in a wholly unofficial capacity. I hadn't been drawing any salary from the government and therefore was a free agent. The companies with which I was associated had been willing to lend me to Mr. Truman temporarily. They were still providing me with a comfortable income. They also were making it virtually impossible for their executives to do any business with the government.

As long as I was attached to the White House, it was

necessary for them not to place themselves in the position of accepting any favors—or anything that looked like a favor—from the Administration. I was an actual liability to them in the White House. Yet they were willing to leave me there at the President's pleasure because—no sophisticate will ever believe this—they are patriotic men. It was as simple as that and as unbelievable to the critics of American society who always proceed from the premise that a successful businessman is necessarily a grasping grubber, if not actually a crook.

There was much speculation while I was in the White House but not on the government payroll about what I was doing there for my business associates. But it didn't bother me very much because I knew I was doing nothing for them—and that nobody, therefore, could ever prove that I was. In fact, I rather enjoyed being "the mystery man." And I was able to keep out of sight enough to prevent suspicious comment from becoming an embarrassment to the Truman Administration.

If I went to the RFC as a director, I would have to shed the protective cloak of mystery, accept a government salary of $10,000 a year, and submit myself and my record to examination by the United States Senate. Since the Senate had confirmed me three times for District Commissioner—always without dissent—I wasn't much concerned about another examination by this august body. What I forgot was that the District Commissionership was only a job but that an RFC directorship was regarded as a plum—and a plum that could be squeezed for the ben-

efit of constituents seeking plum juice in the form of
loans. A would-be borrower is in much better shape if he
can file a Senator with his loan application. I had friends
in the Senate, but I also had acquaintances who wouldn't
regard me as a squeezable plum.

What I should have expected—but in my innocence did
not—was the outcry in the press against my confirmation.
If I had ever entertained any illusions about my character
and capacities (and I had), they were now stripped from
me by the columnists and commentators. I became a man
possessed of neither integrity nor intelligence. I became
a scandal. It is a strange sensation, being a public scandal.
I read the columns and I began to be outraged myself at
this ridiculous appointment of a man without a vestige of
qualification for the job. It was difficult to remember at
times that they were talking about me, George Allen, a
fellow for whom I personally had the highest regard.

Some of my favorite publications denounced me. Some
of the columnists I had been reading for years, but never
in my life had seen, seemed to know me well. They told
their readers just what kind of disgrace to the Administration and country my appointment was. Some of them
called me a clown, but always I was a sinister clown. The
firecracker I used in my act was a bomb capable of blowing up the government itself.

They were outraged, too, by Truman's nomination of
Jake Vardaman for a place on the Federal Reserve Board
and of Edwin Pauley for Under Secretary of the Navy.

But I gathered, with some reverse English pride, that I was even more dangerous than these two Presidential cronies. The Kiplinger Letter predicted, placing the evils in their proper relationship, that the Senate would confirm Pauley reluctantly but reject me—the reverse of what it ultimately did. Harold Ickes, himself a columnist by this time, ran a column inspiring the headline in the *Washington Star*: "Appointment of Allen to RFC Board Called Worst Choice Made by Truman." Here are some of the other comments:

Walter Lippmann: "It is a disagreeable business to have to challenge two men as close as Pauley and Allen to the President of the United States but the alternative is more disagreeable. It is to admit that after this war and other wars, after the Civil War, indeed every other war, the standard of public morals must for a time inevitably fall. We cannot admit this must happen. But it has been happening in Washington, and once the deterioration of standards sets in, things go not from good enough to bad, but from bad to worse, as they did under Grant and Harding. So this is the time, and here's the occasion for the responsible leaders of the Democratic party to take a stand and compel the President to see before it is too late where blind friendship is taking him."

The New Republic: "President Truman's White House career to date has been studded with bad appointments, but last week he sent two nominations [Allen and Pauley] to the Senate which give real cause for national concern. In nominating these two men, the President has shown a scandalous disregard for his public trust. Every effort should be made to block their confirmation."

St. Louis Post-Dispatch: "President Truman's appointment of George Allen as Director of the RFC with the expectation that he will become its chairman elevates to a position of tremendous power and responsibility a man with almost no qualifications for the job."

Drew Pearson: "George Allen is the kind of person anyone likes to have around. He never gets irked, keeps everyone in good humor, works day and night for his chief. Nevertheless, he represents a dangerous influence in government, especially when sitting in such a key post as the RFC."

The *New York Post*: "One has the feeling that a poorer and poorer cast is dealing desperately with a bigger and bigger story. Hopkins dead, Ickes gone, and their replacements are men like Pauley and George E. Allen."

The *Chicago Daily News*: "It would require a diligent search to uncover his qualifications for the RFC assignment."

George Sokolsky: "Mr. Allen has no experience to justify him holding such a position."

Frank Kent: "Another little incident that reflects no credit on the Senate was the way which one of its committees let George Allen, whom the President had named as RFC director, clown himself into the job."

These samples indicate the sweep of opinion against my nomination. It cut across party lines and political prejudices in a remarkable way. I can't remember George Sokolsky, Drew Pearson, and Frank Kent, for example, ever before or since in such cozy agreement. The New Dealers thought I was dragging down the Administration's tone. The anti-New Dealers, who considered the tone already low, thought my appointment took it down still another register.

There were, it is true, a few dissenting voices—writers who thought I wasn't so bad. But they were drowned out by the chorus of dismay. I shan't bother to quote them here. To do so would be pleasant, but it would distort the picture by making it appear that there were two more or less equally divided schools of journalistic thought about my nomination. Actually, it was about ninety-nine to one.

Just how such a pipsqueak as I turned out to be could also become a major scandal was one of the incongruities of the episode, but nobody bothered to notice it except me. The Senate, of course, paid some attention to the opinions of the journalists. Vardaman and I were called before the Senate Banking and Currency Committee to explain, if we could, how we qualified for offices of high responsibility in the United States government. By the time it came my turn to testify I had just about been convinced by the advance billings that my qualifications were too insignificant to mention.

Yet I couldn't very well say: "Why don't you fellows just report that I'm unqualified and get it over with?" I was carrying Truman's colors and had to make a run for it. His attitude was that my critics weren't after me—

that they were sniping at him through me. What they were saying, to his mind, was that Truman couldn't pick a good man for the RFC, that Allen was a bad choice only because he was Truman's choice. Rationalizations of that kind, however much or little there may be in them, are what endear Truman to his subordinates.

No, I had to go through with it. My friends all gave me advice about how to conduct myself before the committee. It was good advice. Don't, whatever the provocation, be funny, they said. Be deadly serious. Be pompous. Be outraged by any question of moral or intellectual fitness. It was good advice because Congressmen like stuffed shirts, just as the voters do. Americans don't mind having public officials they can laugh at, but they hate having public officials they suspect of laughing back at them.

I answered my summons to appear before the Banking and Currency Committee early in 1946. Vardaman was also on hand. The hearing room in the Senate Office Building was packed. The press occupied two long tables. Senator Robert A. Taft thumbed through a pile of papers in happy anticipation of something—my dismemberment, I presumed. I reviewed my life quickly, wondering which of my sins could be recorded at such great length in Taft's pile of documents.

Excuses for various peccadilloes formed in my mind. "But I was so very young then—not more than forty," I said to myself, rehearsing what I would say to Taft. "All that was before I had grown up and learned how careful a fellow must be about picking up with strangers who may turn out to be bad influences on an otherwise blame-less youth."

I remember that Steve Early, who at that time was not in government, occupied a prominent seat in the front row of spectators. While I appreciated Steve's moral sup-port, I found myself wishing he hadn't come. What would he think of me after Taft had read from that dossier about my early mistakes? Well, he'd read about it in the papers, anyway. He might as well hear it firsthand from Taft. Most of the others were people I didn't know. Many of them were eager-looking women, leaning forward in their seats. All they needed was knitting to look to me like the women of revolutionary Paris gathered around the guillotine for my beheading.

Finally, Alben Barkley, who was acting as chairman of the committee, called my name. "George E. Allen," he said in a firm voice. That was my name all right. It sur-prised me that he didn't snarl when he intoned it. I noted with some wonder that his voice was kindly. Then I re-membered. Of course. He was a friend of mine. I had a friend there—two friends, Barkley and Steve. I felt a little better.

I was pushing my way to the witness chair when Bark-ley gave me a reprieve. "We shall have to postpone this nomination," Barkley said. "Senator Tobey wants to ask some questions and he can't be here today."

What a relief! But, on second thought, what a letdown! I'd have to gather my forces all over again for the ordeal now merely postponed. And what was this about Senator

Tobey? This was the same Senator Charles Tobey of New Hampshire who was blocking Pauley's nomination before another Senate committee. Vardaman also got a postponement. When his name was called, Senator Forrest Donnell of Missouri, a man who looks much like the old Rollin Kirby conception of Prohibition, jumped to his feet and raised his hand, like Ajax defying the lightning, and orated: "I ask that you hold an investigation of Mr. Vardaman. Several reports have reached my attention. I suggest that you name a subcommittee to make the investigation."

Several other Truman nominees were quickly approved by the committee that day. Among them was Wilson Wyatt, former Mayor of Louisville, to be Housing Administrator. Vardaman and I were the pariahs. I was later to have some troubles with Wyatt.

I went back to the committee room several days later for a second encounter with Taft's dossier. He wanted to know about my business experience, so I told him all about it, including my hotel operations, my District Commissionership, and my more recent connections with private enterprise. Taft's reports, it developed, concerned two episodes I had almost forgotten. One was my part in supporting a Negro housing project in Washington at the behest of Elder Solomon Lightfoot Michaux, an extremely astute Negro evangelist who had been a sensation on radio with his preaching of the old-time religion and his syncopating choir. Harry Butcher and I had helped him get the money for the housing project, and it had been a great success. I told Taft so and added that I was particularly proud of my part in it.

Penetratingly Taft asked me what I had got out of it. I replied truthfully and with dignity that I had been made an honorary deacon in Elder Michaux's tabernacle. The committee members laughed at that. So did the spectators. Even Taft smiled. I was worried. Everything was going wrong. I was not to let anybody be amused. All my friends had agreed on this, and I knew how right they were. From then on things went from bad to worse, to use a phrase of Lippmann coinage.

The other episode Taft had on his mind was an appearance of mine before the Federal Communications Commission. One of the companies I was a director of had purchased the Crosley Corporation sometime earlier, and among the properties it acquired in the package was WLW, a powerful radio station in Cincinnati, Ohio. I had appeared at a hearing on the question of the fitness of the directors to conduct the affairs of the station in the public interest. Since I was one of the directors, I had quite naturally expressed the opinion that we were fit. What Taft wanted to know was whether I hadn't been using my political influence to get a license to operate WLW. I replied that that had been my idea in appearing but that I was afraid I had hurt our cause more than I had helped it.

That was, in fact, my honest opinion. The Communications Commission had leaned over backward in this case not to favor friends of the Administration. Paul Porter, who used to be the commission's chairman, tells a story about Democratic Chairman Bob Hannegan, getting him on the telephone and asking a hearing for a deserving Democrat. "Send him over," Paul said. "We'll give his application fair and impartial consideration." To which Hannegan replied: "To hell with that. I can *make* you give him that. My man needs more than fair and impartial consideration." But that's all Hannegan's friend got and, I'm sure, all we got.

In spite of my determination to be austere, I was reluctantly beginning to have a pretty good time, and members of the committee seemed to be enjoying my cross-examination, too. I testified that I didn't propose to resign my business connections because I wasn't sure Truman would be re-elected and I wanted some place to go if the Republicans came to power and fired me, as of course they would. It is odd that the simple, unadorned, and bluntly stated truth can be so amusing. By now the committee was in stitches.

I was photographed trying awfully hard to cover a smile with my hand. Members of the committee were photographed laughing. From then on it was said that I had kidded the committee into a recommendation to the Senate to confirm me. So help me, that was exactly what I had tried not to do. More than ever, I was typed as the White House jester. I resigned myself to it after that. The committee voted fourteen to five in my favor.

Even Taft made a pretty fair speech about me when the question of confirmation reached the floor. I was hotly defended by Barkley, Scott Lucas, Brien McMahon, and others. Senator William Langer of South Dakota, who said he didn't know me himself but had read in the newspaper *PM* that I didn't amount to much, demanded that my nomination be sent back to the committee. But I was confirmed by a substantial majority of the Senate and joined the Board of the RFC, where I remained for one year, thus keeping my promise to Truman. At the end of the year, I resigned from the RFC and from public life—forever, I hope.

My hitch at the RFC was not very eventful. I was recognized there, I think it only candid of me to say, as President Truman's emissary. The agency loaned millions of dollars while I was there. The cynical will jump at the conclusion that many of these millions were loaned to the friends, political, if not personal, of Truman—that it was my function to see that this was the case. Examination of the facts, however, would not sustain any part of such a conclusion. I can honestly say that politics was not a consideration in any loan I approved. The only instructions I ever got from Truman were to see that the RFC operated honestly and effectively, making loans where they would do the national economy the most good.

My function was the opposite of what my newspaper critics said it would be. As one who understood government, Truman knew that such agencies as the RFC were potential sources of scandal—that such agencies could easily play favorites. As the chief investigator of war contracting, he also knew American business—particularly the part that dealt most with government. He wanted a personal friend, whom he trusted, to be his watchdog at the RFC. I was it.

Perhaps the one spectacular incident of my incumbency will illustrate my point. It concerned the attempt of Carl Gunnard Strandlund to get a large RFC loan for the production of prefabricated steel houses on a grand scale. Strandlund had interested Housing Administrator Wilson Wyatt, an attractive young Democratic official originally recommended to Truman by Dorothy Rosenman. She was Sam's wife, and a housing enthusiast. There was a critical housing shortage, and Truman wanted to do something about it. Wyatt thought Strandlund's project, the Lustron house, was the answer. He supported Strandlund's demand for a $52,000,000 loan from the RFC. After persuading the War Assets Administration to lease Lustron the wartime Curtiss-Wright plant in Columbus, Ohio, Wyatt came to me. Here let me turn the story over to *Fortune* magazine, which told my part in it more objectively—which is to say more favorably to me— than I could do it.

"Right away," said *Fortune*, "Wyatt bumped into George Allen, the shrewd politician, mistakenly called the White House jester, then head of the RFC." (*A penetrating analysis,* italics mine.) "Allen smiled fondly at Wyatt and Strandlund, listened closely to their request for $52,000,000, and then asked, 'Where are the assets?' This was a stopper. If there was one thing Strandlund was fresh out of, it was assets. Allen took pity and told him that as a special favor, what with the housing crisis and all, he would reconsider the loan if Strandlund would raise $3,600,000; that little ought to be easy."

To shorten *Fortune's* story, the magazine stated that Strandlund invested $1000 himself and sold $840,000 worth of stock to others. That didn't meet my condition, so I turned down the loan.

"Wyatt, undiscouraged," *Fortune* continued, "decided to force the issue with a showdown at the White House. He lost. George Allen burned to keep clean his record of never having made a bad investment—at least away from the race track. The two were photographed shaking hands outside the White House; shortly afterward, giving Lustron as the reason, Wyatt resigned and returned to private life. George Allen, his record clear, resigned a few weeks later."

I repeat that I resigned only after keeping my agreement to remain for a year. Several columnists agreed that I had wrecked veterans' housing—that their worst fears of me had been justified. After I left the RFC it invested $37,500,000 in the Lustron Company, which eventually stumbled into insolvency without justifying the high hopes held for it. I certainly don't complain about what the RFC did. I only make the point that my record in this matter, as in other RFC affairs, was the record of a man who had no qualifications for the job except the political patronage of Truman. Nobody cares, I suppose, except me—and I don't care very much.

Maybe there's a moral beyond self-justification in all

this. I'll look for it a little later. If I find it, the persistent reader of this chronicle will have it rammed down his throat.

In the course of my career as a government banker, I also made a trip to Germany with Assistant Secretary of War Howard Peterson. Our object was to look for ways of encouraging German industry to put the American Occupation Zone on a self-sustaining basis and get it off the American taxpayer's neck. We thought we found some German products that would sell readily in the American market without competing too directly with home products. But our projects became so involved with over-all world diplomatic and political problems that nothing much came of them—at least not immediately.

We arrived in Nuremberg the day Hermann Göring committed suicide and ten other Nazi war criminals were hanged. From Nuremberg we proceeded to Vienna and had to go thirty miles out of our way getting there because the Russians refused to let us travel in their zone, although they placed a whole train at our disposal to travel through it to Salzburg, Austria. It was the first direct experience I had with what often seems to be the utter craziness of Russian diplomacy.

About a year after this trip, I was standing in a hotel lobby in New York during an American Legion Convention when approached by a good-looking young man with a ruptured duck in his buttonhole. He said: "Mr. Allen, you don't remember me, but I was an officer assigned to you and Secretary Peterson while you were in Vienna. I was with Military Intelligence, and we had received word that the diehard Nazis intended to retaliate for the hangings by killing some American brass. We were told that you and Peterson were the chosen victims."

Strangely interested, I asked him some questions.

"You probably don't remember that I pointed my gun at a group of people while escorting you through downtown Vienna one day," he said. "I thought the assassins were in that group."

Just then a playful Legionnaire exploded a firecracker behind me, and I almost jumped through the ceiling.

Since leaving the RFC, I have never considered returning to public office. And every time I read of a new Presidential appointment I bow my head in silent prayer for the poor fellow getting it. He will work harder than he ever worked before in his life, and his reward, unless he is remarkably lucky, will be a lampooning in the press and the disdain of his fellow citizens.

Even the notoriety that comes to him as a public official will be discouragingly limited and transitory. At the height of what I like to regard as my fame, I was cruelly disillusioned. Listening to the radio one Sunday afternoon I heard the Quiz Kids, who knew everything, handle this one from Quiz Master Joe Kelly: "You all know who George Burns and Gracie Allen are. But who are Gracie Burns and George Allen?" They all knew that Gracie Allen was George Burns' wife, but the identity of

George Allen stumped them. Joel Kupperman, making a desperate guess, ventured: "Center fielder for the Chicago Cubs."

But nevertheless, a man may learn something from public affairs and he may even enjoy it, if he lives through the ordeal. I'm sure my character benefited from my public service. Indeed, it got so robust that I plan to spend the rest of my life neglecting it.

CHAPTER 16

Juice

OUT West, where originality of thought and expression persists in spite of the standardizing influence of chain newspapers, radio, movies, and television, they call political influence "juice." A citizen possessed of juice in his home town can telephone the chief of police and say: "Hello, Joe. This is Bill. Howarya, Joe? That's good. I'm fine. You know what a damn fool my wife is, Joe. Well, she parked in front of the fireplug at Main and First at noon today and got a ticket. You'll fix it? Fine, Joe. Thanks, Joe. I'll be seeing ya, Joe. Good-by, Joe."

Bill is a man with juice, and here he used it in the simplest kind of transaction in which juice serves as illegal tender. In Washington, where we are fancier, or perhaps only more standardized in our choice of words, we would call this transaction exercise of influence at the local level.

In a city where the government orders the illumination to be extinguished in government buildings when it merely wants to put out the lights, juice is too short and simple a word to describe a politico-social phenomenon that reformers consider a problem—a problem out of which they make a production.

For this transaction was strictly outside the law. It cheated the people of Bill's town out of a two-dollar fine. It was unjust to every juiceless member of the community who pays two dollars every time his wife, who may be just as much a damned fool as Bill's, parks in front of the fireplug at Main and First.

In my early twenties, when I didn't have so much as an eyedropperful of juice in me, I was capable of becoming righteously indignant, even furious, at this kind of injustice. But in my middle thirties, when I became a District of Columbia Commissioner, I fixed tickets for any Congressman who asked me to—and many did. Anybody who had a vote in Congress and thus a vote that could be cast for or against any District of Columbia appropriation I might recommend had all the juice required to get me to fix a parking ticket. I would even fix speeding tickets. I fixed several of them for Congressman Zioncheck of Washington State, even though his habitual reckless driving was becoming a hazard to the life and limb of District citizens. Finally, it is true, I had him locked up in Gallinger Hospital, Washington's Bellevue, the government's mental hospital, probably in violation of his Constitutional immunity, but that was not until much later, after he had taken to going swimming in the city's fountains and just before the unfortunate fellow committed suicide.

What accounted for the difference between the righteous wrath of my twenties and the corrupt tolerance of my middle thirties? Was it just that my moral sense had been blunted? Or was it that I had compromised with reality? Or is this only another way of saying about the same thing? Or do I bore you with all this moralizing?

Whatever the answers to all these questions, I am now old enough to know that the kind of juice Bill has is possessed by thousands of Americans and used by them daily in hundreds of American communities. I also know that employment of juice by the privileged to circumvent the law in small ways is a practice that will survive thousands of reform administrations and persist, in fact, while these administrations are in power. It is a cliché, but it is also a truism that, as Lord Acton, a distinguished British political philosopher said, power corrupts and that absolute power corrupts absolutely. The fortunate thing for America is that under our system nobody ever achieves absolute power and that we therefore do not become absolutely corrupt.

I am a little ashamed to confess that petty corruption doesn't shock me very much, because in my cynical middle age I have come to think of it as inevitable. If I were shocked by evils I consider inevitable I wouldn't like myself, my fellow men, or the world I live in, and that would leave me in a most unpleasant predicament. I shall concede at once my moral inferiority to my youthful self and proceed to tell you how evil I and my contemporaries are, without bothering to apologize for it as I go along. So I ask the sensitive reader, at this point, to hold onto his hat while I tell him the plain truth: that juice, by other names, also is used in Washington, seat of the greatest democracy the world has ever known.

Some people, if they bother to think about it at all, might think I'm a big Washington juice man myself. Even a few of my friends, who should know better, still think so. My business associates, unfortunately for me, don't embrace this fallacy. I wish they did. If they thought I had a lot of influence in Washington they'd pay me more than they do. To the casual observer, I am a friend of the President, who is boss of the government, and therefore all Washington doors must be open to me. And there must be gold behind them thar doors—government contracts, credit, and other valuable favors.

It is true that many Washington doors are open to me not only because I know the President but because I'm also a friend of many of the people behind those doors. But it is precisely because I am a friend that I must not be given favors. It is precisely because I play golf with these officials, that I go to the races with them and play bridge with them, that I would not, if I could, ask them for any special consideration.

The companies with which I am associated sometimes have business to do with the government, as almost every American company does these days. I am able to tell my associates whom to do business with, how to make their way through the maze of red tape, and how best to conduct themselves, but I can't make a better deal for them with the United States government than any one of their competitors can make.

I haven't that kind of juice. The whole area of influence on government, sometimes called lobbying, is remarkably little explored. It is a twilight zone in which few know their way. Important as it is in the whole scheme of things, it has largely escaped the understanding of journalists and scholars alike. Maybe, as one who has long been an interested observer in this murky territory, I can shed a little light.

To know anything about the terrain in this area, one must first understand that the hills are too rocky to be scaled by friendship. If I wanted to influence the policy of the Federal government in any important way, I would much rather be the enemy than the friend of the President and the party in power. A Federal official is much more likely to give ground to a critic or potential critic than to a friend whose loyalty can be counted upon. In these hills, threat is a more effective alpenstock than friendship.

The most powerful lobbyist Washington has known in my time was Bishop Cannon, head of the prohibition forces. He was enthusiastically disliked by almost all Congressmen, but he was also greatly feared by many. Congressmen will occasionally do little favors for their friends, but they will do big things for their enemies.

What most Congressmen want, above all else, is re-election or promotion in the public service. They respond to the people who can bring them votes or deprive them of votes. With a few exceptions, like Congressmen Andrew May and J. Parnell Thomas, they are not corruptible in any lesser way. They will sometimes go along with policies they don't believe in personally for votes but almost never for any other kind of gain. Some consider this corruption; others call it response to the will of the people and therefore democracy in action.

Henry Ashurst, the great former Senator from Arizona, once made a tremendously impressive fight for a cause he believed in and thought dear to the hearts of his constituents. He invoked the Prophets, Shakespeare, Dante, and a score of lesser thinkers to make his oratorical points. But when the roll call came, he quietly voted against the cause he had defended. One of the Senators who had opposed him in debate grasped his hand and congratulated him on his shift. "Thank God, Henry, you have seen the light," said his colleague. "Oh, no," Ashurst replied. "I didn't see the light. I felt the heat."

Ashurst had been persuaded that the people of Arizona, his constituents, were against the cause he believed in. He had become convinced that it would be hard for him to be re-elected if he persisted in the course he was following. The Senator, who frequently boasted that the clammy hand of consistency—the enemy of progress—never rested long upon his shoulder, didn't hesitate to turn against himself in response to the heat of home opinion.

So it is with most Senators and Representatives. What they want is continuity in office. What they get from continuity is seniority. And what they get with seniority is the committee assignments that give them power. The work of Congress is done principally in committee, and that is where power can be exercised. What most men in Federal government want—whether in the legislative, the executive, or the judicial branch—is power. That comes, in the last analysis, from votes. People who think the mighty in Washington can be persuaded, or corrupted, if you will, by anything less than votes just don't understand what it's all about and never will. They don't know what Washington juice is made of. The kind of juice it takes to fix a ticket back home won't have any effect whatever on an income-tax rap by the Treasury or on Congressional deliberations over a change in the income-tax law or on interpretation of the income-tax law by the United States Supreme Court.

Washington lobbyists are precisely as effective as the number of votes they can deliver outside of Washington on election day. That is why every effort to investigate and regulate them has been principally an exercise in futility. Labor's lobby is today the most effective in the capital, for the obvious reason that labor unions represent millions of votes that are more or less controlled by a unified labor leadership. There isn't any millionaires' lobby in Washington, and if there were it would be the weakest of all, for the simple reason that there are so few millionaire votes. Recently there has been a lot of talk about the landlords' lobby, which is supposed to be devilishly clever and influential, but I notice that rent control, the thing it is supposed to oppose with all its great cunning, somehow manages to remain on the statute books, where the labor lobby wants it.

It is likely that most Congressmen and Senators personally think the wartime necessity for rent control is about over and that the time has come to let the law of supply and demand operate again in the housing business. But majorities in both branches of Congress respond to pressure from the labor lobbies and to statistics indicating that more of their constituents are renters than landlords. So these majorities are corrupted by their hunger for votes and power. And I don't get very indignant about that, perhaps because I don't know many starving landlords or perhaps because I am so inured to injustice and so corrupted by years of unavoidable compromise with the facts of life and government that I don't react as I should to the frustrated intentions of the Founding Fathers. They were pretty conservative about property rights.

The Founding Fathers were never treated with less filial respect than they were in the late Roosevelt and early Truman days by the development of public-opinion polls, which were presumed to reveal month by month, week by week, and almost day by day precisely how a majority of voters felt about every public issue. It began to seem that the representative system of government had become as obsolete as the player piano.

Why should the President, Congress, or, for that matter, the Supreme Court worry their heads about knotty public problems and thresh out decisions of their own? George Gallup, Elmo Roper, and other pollsters could simply ask the sovereign people whether they thought the United States should or should not break off diplomatic relations with Guatemala. If a majority of the voters said yes, then the President could send a telegram calling the United States envoy in Guatemala home, Congressmen could make speeches praising this statesman-like act, and the Supreme Court could get on the band-wagon by handing down a few obiter dicta of approval in some decision otherwise concerned with riparian rights in Iowa.

It made the business of democratic government very simple. What if most of the people polled didn't care how things were in Guatemala? Once they had spoken on this, or any other subject, a democratic decision had been made, and who was a mere politician, their servant, to reverse them?

Not only did the polls tell how the American people as a whole felt about everything, but, more important, from the standpoint of Congressmen and Senators, how their own constituents divided. They could courageously defy the national will if their own people dissented from it and thus maintain the fiction that they were exercising their own independent judgments on public questions.

At one time it seemed that the traditional American system was being revolutionized: that we were going to have government by poll. To be sure, a few traditionalists refused to believe that the polls were always accurate, particularly when these traditionalists disagreed with the decisions the pollsters reported. But almost everyone believed in the polls, including me, when the decisions corresponded with their own prejudices.

President Truman was one of the exceptions. At a time when he was eighty-five per cent popular he questioned whether this was possible. Then, when he dropped to thirty-two per cent, as he once did, he had every right to question the figure.

Government by poll was stopped in its tracks by the election of 1948. The pollsters agreed that Dewey was in— that it was just a question of the landslide's extent. When Truman won, American government reverted overnight to the old system, under which politicians were forced to exercise their own judgment about what policies were right for the country and what policies, right or wrong, or partly right and partly wrong, could be sold to the voters. Politics became an art again, not just a copybook tracing game.

Actually the polls hadn't been very far wrong per-centagewise in 1948—just wrong enough to choose the wrong winner. Gallup was only 4.7 per cent pregnant.

Gallup was once told by a dinner partner that she had never been approached by one of his representatives and asked why. He explained to her that by the law of averages under which his sampling system worked she had about as much chance of being interviewed as she had of being struck by lightning. "But I've been struck by lightning," she objected.

The polls, in their heyday, made lobbyists almost as obsolete as statesmen. Why try to persuade a Congressman that his constituents favored a given piece of legislation if the polls showed otherwise or, indeed, if the polls confirmed the lobbyist's contention?

So the lobbyist, as well as the statesman, was saved by the 1948 reversal.

Still, the lobbyists themselves—the Pressure Boys—don't amount to much these days. They have been forced to register, to tell whom they represent and how much they earn, all of which is demeaning in itself. Senator Hugo Black of Alabama managed to make them sound excitingly sinister for a short time while investigating the power industry's Washington representatives and probably owes his place in the Supreme Court in part at least to that achievement.

Recently there was a brief flare-up over five-percenters and, as a result, John Maragon, a pleasant fellow who knew Major General Harry Vaughan and didn't make any secret of it, went to jail for belittling his achievements too enthusiastically before a Senate committee. Now and then somebody gets indignant about all the money Tommy Corcoran is supposed to be making as a Washington lawyer who has managed to build bridges—or at least get credit for building them—between his former New Deal colleagues in the government and *nouveaux* industrialists like Henry Kaiser.

But I don't get very excited about these things. As I followed Maragon's trial in the newspapers, I noticed that none of his clients ever got anything Maragon had set out to get him. And Tom Corcoran doubtless has contributed heavily to the nation's production by showing businessmen that his friends in the government don't wear horns, and vice versa. Moreover, I seem to remember something in the Constitution about right of petition, and I don't quite see how Washington representatives of various groups of citizens exercising this right can be deported or, for that matter, why they should be. In the long run, one set of lobbyists tends to offset another. The radical pressure boys are checked by the natural conservatism and inertia of elected legislators. And the conservative lobbies are outnumbered and often outgeneraled by the laborites. The consequent balance may not be perfect, but no man-made arrangements are.

Moreover, the presence of lobbyists in the capital gives crusading newspapers like the *St. Louis Post-Dispatch* something to crusade about. I am fond of the *Post-Dispatch*'s crusades, particularly against predatory property interests, which would be very lucky if they could own as much property and make as nice a profit as the *St.*

Louis Post-Dispatch, in which I should like to own some stock.

Those who complain most bitterly about the juice spread around Washington by lobbyists are the columnists and radio commentators, themselves the real juice men of our time. They have tremendous power and they don't all use it with reasonable restraint, although many do. Because their columns are syndicated and their comments are carried over widespread networks, they speak directly and regularly to thousands of voters. Many of them have audiences infinitely larger than any except the very top-flight government officials can reach. These radio and newspaper juicers speak to their audiences every day, whereas government officials are necessarily limited to occasional press conferences and speeches.

Like the lobbyists, the columnists tend to offset each other because they fight among themselves. Recently, for example, Drew Pearson, who has a syndicated newspaper column as well as a widely disseminated weekly radio broadcast and one of the largest regular audiences in the world, filed a libel suit against Westbrook Pegler, who confines his efforts to a vehement newspaper column. This seems to me healthy. My feeling about this suit is somewhat akin to that of the husband whose wife got into a fight with a bear. The husband watched this contest with interest but refused to intervene. Later when his wife took him to task for this refusal, he explained that his own attitude toward the encounter couldn't have been more neutral.

Pearson was the columnist whose operations I followed most closely while in the government. They are fascinating. They had purpose and pattern and were shrewdly designed to exploit the weaknesses of the genus public official. In the morning when I picked up my *Washington Post* I would find an item in the Pearson column poking me, but quite gently, in some vulnerable spot. That afternoon a smiling young man, one of Pearson's employees, would turn up in my office, wondering what news items I had for him that day. It seemed to me that the plain implication of his attitude always was that if I co-operated I would get good publicity in the Pearson columns and broadcasts and if I didn't I would find myself more accurately described to the Pearson audience. Readers addicted to Pearson's daily exposures may easily judge how co-operative I was by the press he gave me. But officials politically ambitious would hesitate to rebuff the Pearson approaches, considering the method a sort of whitemail. It works with a remarkably large number of Washington officials.

The punishment for nonco-operation with Pearson can be quite terrible, as many public officials have found. The late Secretary of the Navy James Forrestal was furiously pursued by Pearson. On one occasion, even his personal courage was assailed. Robert Jones of the Federal Communications Commission was "exposed" as a member of the Black Legion in Pearson's effort to prevent his confirmation by the Senate. When called upon to prove his charge against Jones, Pearson produced as sorry a set of witnesses as anyone has ever assembled in Washington.

While interested in the Pearson method, I was once invited to write a guest column for Austine Cassini in the *Washington Times-Herald*. It began:

> Columnists being the new lords of creation, I count it a real privilege to be called upon to fill the space when, on the seventh day, one of them rests. . . . Let who will write the nation's songs, if I can write its columns. But since I can't write its columns, I must be content to write just this one column.

But because it was a rule of the *Times-Herald* that Pearson's name could not be mentioned in its columns, I wrote about a mythical columnist named Pere Drewson. The late Mrs. Eleanor Patterson, publisher of the paper, who had once been Pearson's mother-in-law, sometimes created the impression that she wasn't very fond of him. I wrote that if I were as influential as some Washington columnists thought I was, I'd write a perfectly impartial law abolishing the Drewson column. The column went on:

> This would be a boon to good government because it would break the Drewson reign of terror, now one of the least inspiring aspects of the Washington spectacle, and give officials time and energy for their work.
>
> Any similarity between this character of my imagina-

tion and any person living or dead, remember, is as much coincidental as any relationship between what happens in Washington and what Drewson writes about what happens in Washington.

This Drewson wears a long black mustache and carries a blacksnake whip. When a new official turns up in Washington, Drewson suggests to this official that he take shorthand notes on his celluloid cuffs of all secret high-policy conferences to which he is admitted and then shoot the cuffs to Drewson.

If the new man complies, Drewson strokes his mustache benignly and writes an open letter to his relatives, and to his other billions of trusting readers, that this new official is a stouthearted liberal, a man of the people, and smart as a snap brim up in front and down behind.

If the new man refuses, Drewson cracks his blacksnake and reports to his avid billions that the official is a reactionary, a lug, a thief, and probably a member of the Hooded Order of Bluebeard Wife Beaters— somebody Congress ought to investigate.

At this stage the new man must be most careful not to offend his stenographer, lest she deliver the secret files, containing Aunt Nelly's tattletale-gray skeleton, to Drewson for rattling over a nation-wide hookup.

At that, Drewson makes things pretty exciting. Of all the versions of my own government service and return to private life, I rather liked Drewson's best. It had a fascinating quality of fantasy about it—and action. I was practically pitched out of the White House.

That sort of thing takes experience and training.

In contrast, Harold Ickes has convinced me that no government official, however much he yearns for the columnist's enviable position of power without responsibility, should try to achieve it. Shelley must have anticipated Harold's column when he wrote *Peter Bell the Third:*

> *Peter was dull—he was at first*
> *Dull—oh, so dull—so very dull!*
> *Whether he talked, wrote, or rehearsed—*
> *Still with this dulness was he cursed—*
> *Dull—beyond all conception—dull.*

Actually, of course, I wouldn't abolish the Pearson column if I could. It sometimes serves the public interest, as when it exposed Congressman Thomas' shakedown of his employees and when it sponsored Friendship Trains for Europe. Also, he and I belong to the same college fraternity, Kappa Sigma, and therefore have a solemn obligation to be fraternal. And when Pearson gets too rough, there are others to set the record straight. As for Ickes, he has now written himself out of his newspaper column, and I am sorry about that. Some of his curmudgeoning was almost entertaining.

In the bulk, the columnists and commentators do an

excellent job of informing the American people about what happens in Washington. Some of them have a very direct influence on government policy. The State Department, whoever heads it, listens to Walter Lippmann and, I trust, understands what he is saying from day to day. That gives me a comfortable feeling because it seems to me that Lippmann changes his mind so often that a State Department following his advice must, in time, hit upon the right policies by a process of steady elimination of old policies.

Personally, I have always found the Washington press corps alert to a fault and often amusing. I lived with some of its members off and on while working for President Truman and found them generous about lending me toothpaste and shaving cream. Once at Caruthersville, Missouri, on a junket that got Mr. Truman more bad publicity than I thought reasonable, we even got the gentlemen of the press to attend church on a Sunday morning. It was the First Baptist Church of Caruthersville, and on that Sunday it had a printed "Order of Worship." One of the numbers was a solo, *I Had a Little Talk with the Lord*, by a member of the choir named George Allen.

I was no more than settled in the pew when I received a note from Bill Hillman of *Collier's* calling attention to the solo and saying: "I want the first quote." Yes, the Fourth Estate is on its toes, and the Republic is safe.

CHAPTER 17

I'd Rather Be Occupied
by Yankees

I AM indebted to Palmer Hoyt, editor and publisher of
the *Denver Post*, for a story about early American politics
that somehow has been overlooked by the authors of
textbooks used in our schools. It is a great pity that this
story is not better known. While perfectly true in itself
and as such susceptible of documentation, it also has
about it some of the quality of the parable. We Americans do not have enough political parables. The story
of George Washington and the cherry tree illustrates
the virtue of veracity and is perfectly all right as far as
it goes, but Parson Weems was not a man of broad
enough imagination to enrich our folklore with truly
great stories about the father of our country.

The lore of Abraham Lincoln is better. Take, for example, Lincoln's comment on the problem of the curl in the pig's tail: "I could never quite understand why the Lord put a curl in a pig's tail. It never seemed to me to be either useful or ornamental, but I reckon that the Almighty knew what He was doing when He put it there, and as it is outside my department, I have quit fretting about it." This comment tells us much about Lincoln's sense of proportion, his observation and willingness to abdicate to higher authority in a matter involving no great moral principle.

My story—or rather Hoyt's story—has to do with a party of men from Utah who set out on a gold-prospecting expedition in December, 1873, in the San Juan mountains. After suffering hardship and privation, they reached the camp of Chief Ouray of the Ute Indians, who told them, in effect, that they were silly to travel in winter and might as well remain with him until spring. Most of them, being reasonable men and already very cold, thought Chief Ouray's idea fundamentally sound. But six of the band—Packer, Bell, Humphrey, Swan, Noon, and Miller—were still full of American enterprise and said they'd press on to the gold fields without further waste of precious time.

Six weeks later Packer turned up alone at the Los Pinos agency, seventy-five miles from Lake City, complaining that he had gone lame and been deserted by his no-account, though still enterprising, companions. He had been subsisting, he said, on roots and small game.

But apparently roots and small game had agreed with him remarkably because he was bursting with health and his first request was for whisky rather than food. The agency people told each other that this Packer was quite a man, yes, sir, quite a man, and were sorry when his restless spirit urged him on to Saguache, a community some distance away.

Although Packer had claimed to be broke while in Los Pinos, he seemed to have come by some drinking and gambling money by the time he arrived in Saguache.

Meanwhile an Indian had arrived at the agency with strips of flesh he said he'd picked up along Packer's trail. And that spring, after the snows had melted, a photographer for *Harper's Weekly*, crossing the plateau, stumbled upon the remains of five men whose skulls had been crushed and whose bodies had been partially stripped of their flesh. Packer was in trouble, but had an explanation. He said he had been forced to kill Bell, who went insane, in self-defense, and later found that Bell had killed the other four men. The whole episode had been so distasteful, Packer explained, that he couldn't bring himself to talk about it when he first arrived back in civilization.

The Los Pinos agency people wanted to believe Packer but found it so difficult that they arrested him instead. But not having a jail, they chained him to a rock, from which he soon escaped. He was not recaptured until ten years later in Wyoming. Then he was returned to Lake City for trial. By that time, the two-party system was established in Lake City and law and order were rearing their pretty heads. Packer was given an efficient trial and sentenced to be hanged. His trial and sentencing were strictly bipartisan. All jurymen were Republicans, but the Judge, M. B. Gerry, was of the Democratic and minority persuasion. Bringing the trial to a close he shouted:

"Alfred Packer, you man-eating son of a bitch, stand up." When Packer obeyed, the Judge went on: "Alfred Packer, you depraved Republican cannibal, I hereby sentence you to hang by the neck until you are dead. There were only six Democrats in Hinsdale County, and, by God, you've et five of them."

This homily has much to tell us, if we will but study it, and learn from it, about the true nature of American politics. It will be observed, in the first place, that one determined Republican was more than a match in the first instance for five Democrats. That should be some comfort to present-day Republicans, who appear to be outnumbered by about that proportion. But it should warn them, at the same time, never to underestimate the power of a Democrat once he has achieved a position of authority. Note that the political implications of Packer's crime lost nothing in Judge Gerry's pronouncement of sentence. It would be said, if we were saying it today, that he made political capital of Packer's Republican hunger. And the whole story is redolent of the man-eat-man character of what is sometimes called the "political game."

Make no mistake about it, politics is a rough game and it can be played successfully only by the most rugged among us. As for me, during the brief period when I labored in the Washington vineyard, I trembled within myself almost constantly. I awoke fearful of reaching for the morning paper, fearful of what the headline writers, the columnists, and the editorial writers would say of yesterday's mistakes, fearful of what the Republican cannibals would cook up from the bones of yesterday's successes.

But since I've left the government, the morning paper is again a fascinating Pandora's box in which one may find almost anything. As others follow baseball, or the opera, or the movies, I follow politics and politicians. I am a politics fan.

I also follow the horses, but racing is a pale sport compared with politics. A real politician, one who has it in him to work his way to the top and stay there, even for a short time, is a remarkable animal. He must have the hide of a rhinoceros, the kind of intelligence that can guess what a few million voters are going to want in the way of government policy next week and next year and, at the same time, to remember the faces and names of several thousand of them; he must have showmanship of a high order and the heart and stamina of a steeplechaser. It is out of admiration for these qualities that I cultivate politicians. I like and admire them. I like to be with them. They may strut before their constituents, but I have observed that they almost always see through their own pomposities. They are natural-born gamblers, if they are any good at politics, and the stakes they play for are the highest in the world—power over the destinies of other men.

It is axiomatic that businessmen make bad politicians. The recurring cry for honest businessmen in government is the cry of of the hopeless uninitiate. The business executive has only a board of directors to please and employees to worry about. His object is a profit. The politician has hundreds or thousands or millions of constituents to please and nobody to order around except his own secretary and stenographer. All the rest of his associates are rivals. The ultimate end of his endeavor must be the complicated thing called good government. When he climbs up into the political stratosphere of national and international leadership, he is playing not only for the approbation of a majority of the voters of the United States but for a decent, if not highly distinguished, place in history. And even if he becomes, in his lifetime, the idol of millions, he is still only old Moosejaw, the bandit chief, or some equally distasteful thing, to his critics. He must subject not only himself but his family and friends to the kind of vilification that is tolerated nowhere except in the political arena.

Thus politics is the only place where the high art of invective still flourishes. These days actors and actresses who hate each other nevertheless call each other "darling." Politicians, even when they are rivals or bitter enemies in public, often like each other personally but never acknowledge any such emotional weakness. It remains one of America's virtues and national assets that its public men—and most of its private citizens as well—can be friendly political enemies. Most of us aren't sure enough of our own political wisdom to reject the other fellow's arguments out of hand. I am fully aware that the opinions I am expressing so positively here may change day after tomorrow. But the grand insult is still one of the honored traditions of the politician's craft. They aren't as good as they used to be, but they still try.

None of them has ever climbed the heights achieved by Victorian statesmen. But the Victorians had the kind of elegant dignity that punctures best, so this failure is understandable. The classic is, of course, Disraeli's riposte to Gladstone's thrust. Infuriated by Disraeli in Parliamentary debate, Gladstone said: "Mr. Disraeli, you will probably die by the hangman's noose or a vile disease." Disraeli replied: "Sir, that depends upon whether I embrace your principles or your mistress."

Senator John Randolph of Roanoke, Virginia, celebrated for his caustic wit, once said of Senator Henry Clay that, "like a rotten mackerel by moonlight, he shines and stinks." And Andrew Jackson, who was capable of eloquent fury, if not of wit, said upon quitting Washington for the last time: "I have only two regrets: that I didn't have an opportunity to hang Henry Clay and shoot John C. Calhoun."

Senator John Sharp Williams, of Mississippi, a man equally devoted to good talk and good bourbon, once decorated the pages of *The Congressional Record* with sharper words than they display, except on rare occasions, these days. Williams once annoyed Senator Tom Heflin of Alabama with frivolous interruptions in the course of a serious and bombastic speech. Trying to silence his tormentor, Heflin said: "At least, I am in complete command of my faculties." Williams, who had drunk a good lunch, snorted: "What difference does that make?"

More recently one United States Senator said of another: "There's no use telling that fellow anything. It just goes in one head and out the other." And General Carl Spaatz, long before he became famous, said of President Calvin Coolidge: "He thinks things through very carefully before going off half-cocked."

The true politician thoroughly enjoys and appreciates the *mot juste,* even when it is at his own expense and sometimes, indeed, particularly when it is at his own expense. It is an indication that he's still important enough to be hated. Presdent Roosevelt's favorite story was about the commuter from Westchester County, a Republican stronghold, who always walked into his station, handed the newspaper boy a quarter, picked up the *New York Herald Tribune,* glanced at the front page, and then handed it back as he rushed out to catch his train. Finally the newsboy, unable to control his curiosity any longer, asked his customer why he only glanced at the front page.

"I'm interested in the obituary notices," said the customer.

"But they're way over on page twenty-four, and you never look at them," the boy objected.

"Boy, the son of a bitch I'm interested in will be on page one."

Even Governor Thomas E. Dewey, a particular victim of the quipsters, of whom an unpublished book was written entitled *He'd Rather Be President,* is a man with inner resources of humor. He said after the 1948 election, which he had been completely confident of winning, that everyone was kind to him but that he felt like the butt of a practical joke he had heard about.

The joke was on an Irishman who passed out at a particularly tearful and bibulous wake. Thinking to relieve their heavily burdened spirits of the agonies of mourning the departed, the other guests removed the corpse from its coffin and substituted the inert body of the passee. Having done this they went their way feeling better. The understudy for the corpse woke up a few hours later and said to himself: "Well, I must be dead or I wouldn't be in this coffin with this lily in my hand, but if I am dead, why is it that I want to go to the bathroom?"

Incidentally, I have always felt that Governor Dewey conducted his 1948 campaign in the only way he could have to win. All the Republicans who accused him of losing because he "me-tooed" Truman and the Democrats were talking out of the folly of misdirected hindsight. The fact of the matter is that the Democratic party, speaking through the mouths of its two most recent leaders, Roosevelt and Truman, has convinced a majority of Americans that it is the party of the people—the party that has given and will continue to give the majority what it wants.

The Republicans have no chance but to confuse the voters into thinking they are Democrats too, but by another name, or that they have broken completely with their past. Like the Tories in England, who tried to seem more Socialist than the Laborites in the election of early 1950, the Republicans must try to seem more Democratic than the Democrats.

From all this the reader may conclude that I am more interested in politicians than I am in political principles and therefore that I am only a frivolous political philosopher. Such a conclusion would, perhaps, be not too far wrong. Mrs. Allen once commented upon my seriousness as a thinker by picking up a racing form I had dropped out of my pocket and handing it to me with the comment: "Here, dear, you dropped your Kiplinger Letter." On the other hand, Mrs. Allen underrates not only my political sagacity but also my skill as a political practitioner.

She has gone so far, at times, as to accuse me of liking the publicity a politician can't wholly avoid. When we were first married she used to throw our old friend, Tommy Hamilton, then the football coach at Annapolis, in my face. He got more publicity as a coach than I did as a District Commissioner, but Mrs. Allen always insisted that, whereas I sought publicity, he avoided it as much as possible. One morning she triumphantly read me a newspaper article to the effect that Hamilton, having beaten Army for the first time in years, learned while returning from Philadelphia that the midshipmen were planning a great home-coming celebration for him and his team, when they reached Annapolis. To avoid having a fuss made over him, he quietly detrained at Baltimore and sent his team on to receive the kudos. "That's exactly what I or any other reasonably modest person would have done," I answered. "George," said my wife, "you know very well that you would have put the team off at Baltimore."

Publicity is, of course, one of the indispensable tools of the political craftsman. A man in public life deliberately creates a public personality that may bear only the most tenuous relationship to his private personality. He can't, of course, control his publicity, but he can direct it. He creates in his own mind the image of what he wants the public to think about him and then plays up to that image.

Sometimes he fails to be type-cast the way he wants to be—as I did. I became first the gay Commissioner and then the White House Clown. That wasn't deliberate. I would have preferred to be known as an amiable but serious and hard-working Jeffersonian. My trouble was that I wasn't a good enough actor to remain in my chosen character when in the company of the journalists who wrote about me. Once they had the cap and bells adjusted, I could never get rid of them. I know of only one man, in fact, who has completely reversed his public role. Oscar Ewing, Federal Security Administrator, first came to the attention of the public as a Wall Street attorney for the Aluminum Company of America—as a lawyer for a big and presumably evil monopoly. Now he's known as the sponsor of socialized medicine. Ewing's has been, so far as I know, an unparalleled feat of reversal.

It was my misfortune also, while I'm reviewing my own troubles, that I sometimes laughed in the wrong places. I would have been quite incapable of keeping my face composed while delivering the kind of speech I once heard my own Mississippi Congressman make in a hot campaign. He was addressing a farm audience— naturally, since the largest city in his district was less than three thousand—when, striking a pose of leonine ferocity, he said: "I am for free seed for the farmers even if it defeats me."

But when I started this book my idea was that young men and women could read it and then, profiting from my mistakes, start their heavy political thinking and their careers where mine are ending. Now that I approach the conclusion of this literary effort, however, I realize how futile such an attempt to transfer experience is. Everybody has to learn for himself. I started life a firm states' rights Democrat. I was completely convinced that government is best when it governs least. During my radical period in college—the period everybody goes through— I wrote solemn compositions advocating the initiative and referendum and the direct primary. I felt pleasurably subversive in favoring these reforms we now take for granted.

When I come right down to it, I find that about all I have learned in my long career as a political kibitzer and my short interlude as a practicing politician is that I haven't learned very much. That, in itself, is a valuable thing to know. I shall feel that my mission has been accomplished if I can convince others that they don't know the answers, either.

On second thought, maybe I have learned one other thing: that wisdom travels the middle of the road, somewhere between hyperthyroid reformism on the left and stubborn standpatism on the right. Those who advocate change merely for the sake of change and those who advocate the kind of conservatism that insists upon conserving the egregiously bad along with the patently good are equally harebrained. I admire the statesman who can keep to the middle even when exposed to fire from both sides. Often, particularly in turbulent periods, he is a lonely man and to hold his course he must be a brave one. The highest compliment I can pay a politician is to say of him that he is a middle-of-the-roader.

We are living in crazy times. Our world has been turned upside down by the rapid advances of our science —advances that have left the art of government far behind. Our only salvation lies in open-minded adjustment of our social sciences, including political science, to new conditions the pure sciences are creating. The more we avoid rigidity in our thinking and in our law the better off we shall be. Fortunately, our constitutional system, which is about as badly designed as it could be to cope with modern problems, doesn't work the way it is supposed to—the way the Founding Fathers thought it would and the way the textbooks say it does. So far, it has served and served magnificently because its elaborate system of checks and balances has been modified in practice to permit reasonably quick decision and reasonably rapid adjustment to changing needs. Fortunately, too, the Republican and Democratic parties stand for about the same things. Thus, the country faces the dangers of the immediate future basically united and strong.

The Republican and Democratic parties are only formal associations held together by tradition. I am a Democrat principally because I always have been and because that is the team I play on. But I recognize that, as far as political theory is concerned, there isn't as much difference between Senator Harry Byrd of Virginia, leader of the Southern wing of the Democratic party, and Senator Robert Taft of Ohio, leader of a large and probably the dominant segment of the Republican party, as there is between Taft and Senator Wayne Morse of Oregon, nominally a Republican, or between Byrd and lame-duck Senator Claude Pepper of Florida, nominally a Southern Democrat.

I am somewhat amused at the spectacle of James Byrnes of South Carolina, recently trying to build a states' rights party within the Democratic party after serving for years as a Roosevelt leader in the Senate, where he employed his skill as a political craftsman to push through a whole series of measures undermining states' rights. We are fortunate in having many statesmen who, to use the words of wise former Senator Henry Ashurst, are capable of "rising above principle."

I believe these measures were necessary and I don't criticize Byrnes for supporting them. The Federal government during the depression and war years had to use powers formerly reserved to the states. It also had to use powers formerly reserved to private enterprise. In all probability, there never again will be a time when the Federal government can safely surrender all of these powers. Quick transportation and communication have all but obliterated state lines; the complex interdependence of our industrial society has made some degree of Federal control inevitable. Those of us who like individual freedom and are used to it may not like these developments. But we had better get used to lumping them. The clock can't be turned back.

I have no sympathy with people who say that the tendency toward centralization of government, when held within the bounds of dire necessity, is essentially immoral because politicians are essentially immoral. I have known thousands of politicians during my life, including many of the so-called bosses of city machines, yet I have known no more than a half dozen I believed to be dishonest. Politics is just as honest as business—possibly more so, because it is conducted in the open, where all

245

may see and where the shady characters and the shady deals are soon observed and soon eliminated. Observe that Lincoln Steffens, the greatest muckraker of city machines in our time, ended up an admirer of the politicians he had been denouncing. Their operations often were without the law, but when they did lie beyond the pale, Steffens discovered, there was more often than not some good social reason for their extralegal activities.

Experience has led me to believe that the best system of government is that which is least systematic. I believe in pragmatic flexibility. I believe in leeway for the pull and haul of conflicting opinions and conflicting forces. Let the pressure groups exert pressure. One will counteract another. Let ideas clash. Out of the conflict will come a compromise that will be more good than bad.

I have complete confidence that in the world struggle between Soviet Russia and the United States of America, the United States will win in a breeze. I think so not because we have a more highly developed industrial machine and more skilled workers, though these will be factors, but because our minds are not held in bondage by a rigid political philosophy, as the Russian mind is held by Marxism. The Marxian theory of economic determinism, of inevitable class conflict, of inevitable capitalistic wars, is plausible but demonstrably wrong in most of its basic assumptions. People in the mass don't fit any such neat pattern. They never will. And any government dedicated to the proposition that they do must be fundamentally weak.

We are in for a long, hard struggle to protect what is left of the free world from further Communist encroachment. But we can win it and we will win it unless we are stupid enough to listen to the counsel of supercaution from those who say we can't afford to arm ourselves for modern war or to help arm our allies. I like the idea of a balanced budget too, but I'd rather go broke as a nation than go slave as a nation. If I must make a choice I prefer bankruptcy to a Communist concentration camp. Uncle John may turn over in his grave, but I'm going to say it anyway: I'd rather be occupied by Yankees this time than by Russian Communists. And in the long view, this conflict in which we are engaged may be our salvation. In Arnold Toynbee's terms—in his panoramic view of the rise, decline, and fall of civilizations—Russian Communism probably will be the stimulus to which we can respond with growing strength and increasing vitality for generations to come.

Myself, I expect to view this struggle with calm optimism. Fear not, I tell myself; the men who emerge as our leaders will have the incalculable advantage of knowing me.

Index

INDEX